MINISTRY ESSENTIALS

Keys to Church Health

Dr. Michael Brodeur

To a great extent, the individual segments of this book correspond to the Assessment Result Videos featuring Michael Brodeur offered on www.PastorsCoach.com. Visit our website for more information on building your church, creating culture, developing leaders and small groups, etc.

To receive a free email newsletter delivering tips, teachings and updates about Pastor's Coach and our products, register directly at www.PastorsCoach.com.

Pastor's Coach Endorsements

"So appreciate Michael Brodeur and his heart to invest in pastors and leaders. One of the best I know. He's made a huge impact on my own life."

Banning Liebscher
Jesus Culture Director
Sacramento, CA.

"Michael has a unique ability to connect and relate to the real stuff of life and ministry. How I wish that I had a mentor or coach like Michael much earlier in my journey."

Randy Turpin
President, Valor Christian College
Columbus, OH.

"Pastor's Coach is an amazing new organization based in Redding, California designed to help pastors and leaders build thriving churches that transform their cities for Christ."

C. Peter Wagner
Vice President, Global Spheres Inc.

"Michael's Spirit-born insights make him a consummate coach to ministers."

Dr. Leo Lawson
President, ACEA
Chapel Hill, NC.

I work with Michael on a regular basis and I find him to be one of the most effective equippers of church leadership that I know. I travel the world and I regularly find myself recommending, to church leaders who are going through challenges or want to go to the next level, Michael on a consistent basis.

Steve Backlund
Founder, Igniting Hope Ministries
Associate Director, Global Legacy
Redding, CA.

"We have known Michael for over twenty-five years. We love Michael Brodeur, his wisdom, his counsel, and his high-level skill set."

Wesley and Stacey Campbell
Founders, Be a Hero
Founder, Canadian Prophetic Council
Apostolic Team Members, Harvest International Ministries
Founders, New Life Church
Kelowna, B.C., Canada

"Our church is around 1,800 to 2,000 in weekly attendance. It's growing. And, also our Dunamis Movement, our para-church organization, is reaching over 150 university campuses. Most of them in the country of Brazil. So, that being said, I really needed help. I reached out to Michael. He came in with leadership principles. He coached myself and my team. We've been interacting for the last 5 years. And, over the last 5 years, I've seen tremendous growth and health. Health in my staff. Health in my own ministry. I highly, highly recommend Michael Brodeur and the Pastor's Coach team."

Teo Hayashi
Founder, Dunamis Movement
Senior Leader, Mt. Zion Church
Sao Paulo, Brazil

"Michael and Pastor's Coach has just absolutely changed the dynamic of our leadership team. And, helped us get practical steps towards our destiny and towards our purpose. And also, it's totally changed the dynamic of our church where we have so many more people coming into leadership and walking out their destiny and their calling. I can't recommend it highly enough. Amazing. Join. You'll be so glad that you did."

Matt Stutzman
Senior Leader, Church at Baltimore
Baltimore, MD.

"The thing that I've found about working with Michael, Pastor's Coach, so many different things that he's doing and the new website is that it isn't just some material. You can tell the heart of the person that put this material together; they know what their talking about because they know Jesus intimately and they know how to work with people in a way that makes a difference. Check it out."

Fred Bruner
Senior Leader, Hope Church
Casper, WY.

"I heard about Michael because, like many of you, as a pastor I'm always looking for new ways that I can grow as a leader and I can improve the quality of ministry that's happening in my church. And, a fellow pastor recommended Michael. I didn't know him. We just set up a Skype session through email. And, sooner rather than later, we had him come to our church and, let me tell you, he's been such a blessing. He's shown us blind spots, encouraged us in our gifting's, but also showed us places where we can grow and improve. And, I want to tell you, I've seen the results. You're going to see the results as well. So listen, if you're considering letting Michael visit your church or just receiving from Pastor's Coach, I want to give my whole-hearted recommendation. You will not be disappointed. God bless you."

Jeff Struss
Senior Pastor, Revival Scene Community Church
Co-Director, Clear River Network
Lynchburg, VA.

"Using the *Pastor's Coach Church Health Assessment* we were able to see through the eyes of a variety of individuals in our church what the true state of the heartbeat of our church was. We are happy to see we were above average for most of the categories, and now know where to focus our attention."

Marvin Poole
Senior Pastor, The Harbor Church
Hammond LA.

How to Use This Book

Welcome to *Pastor's Coach Ministry Essentials: Keys to Church Health*. This series will help you navigate points of common frustration and issues as a pastor in your church or ministry. The following pages are filled with tips, suggestions, pointers and ideas that will help you troubleshoot the following areas:

- Leadership development
- Outreach
- Discipleship
- Administration
- Supernatural ministry
- And much more

Pastor's Coach Ministry Essentials: Keys to Church Health, addresses the health of your church and will help you nurture your congregation, develop ministries that benefit your congregation and raise up leaders out of your congregation.

Feel free to jump around and use this book as a reference guide. This book has 10 theme statements followed by five focal points that break the themes into bite-sized pieces. You can access the information you need on a case-by-case basis or read the book straight through. Our goal is to help you start thinking in new ways as you build your church and follow God's leading. Please keep in mind this book is not intended to be a complete encyclopedia of church growth and troubleshooting, and if you need more information or coaching in a certain area, please contact us at www.PastorsCoach.com.

Check out our website at www.PastorsCoach.com and explore our different subscription options. You can also utilize our online assessment tools to get a better, deeper picture of where you are as a church, what is going well, what you might need to strengthen, etc. May God bless every step of the journey for you!

CONTENTS

Preface

We are privileged to live in an amazing season in the Body of Christ. The Church has grown to fill the earth, and the number of unreached people groups around the world is diminishing quickly as God moves in incredible ways.

The earth's population just reached 7 billion, and prophets and prognosticators increasingly confirm we are on the verge of a massive great awakening. Many people are prophesying a billion-soul harvest. As followers of Jesus, this could be the greatest time to be alive in all human history—and yet many churches are struggling.

It is time to prepare for what God is about to do, which is the reason Pastor's Coach exists. The Holy Spirit is moving around the earth, reminding us of what is truly important. He is working within us to:

1. Increase our ability to hear the Father's voice,
2. Realign our identities in Him,
3. Help us be at peace within ourselves,
4. Help us build good community and have healthy communication and
5. Bring His Kingdom to the world around us.

At the same time, He is strengthening us to reach the lost, bring them into the family of God and raise them up as spiritual sons and daughters—so *they* can become the leaders God called them to be.

On the one hand, this is a time for rejoicing over all God has done. But on the other hand, we have to take a serious look at the preparation that needs to take place, so we can handle the coming harvest.

The New Reformation

We are entering a season of Kingdom reformation in which every believer will be empowered according to his or her gifts and callings to represent Christ powerfully in the Church and the world beyond. God is restoring the Body of Christ so we can go out and affect the entire earth—not just in the realm of religion but also in government, business, education, medicine and the other facets of human life. Therefore, every member needs to be empowered in every aspect of life. We are called to be representatives of Jesus, salt and light, to shine forth the glory of God in every sphere and bring about transformation. This requires every single member stepping into the true calling of God on his life. That is what we call the *new reformation*.

And this new reformation signals a great shift in the way we "do church."

From time to time throughout history, God has radically reformed His Church, and perhaps the most significant occurrence was 500 years ago in what we call the Protestant Reformation. Martin Luther posted his 95 theses on the Wittenberg door, and the subsequent rediscovery of three primary truths helped shape the next five centuries:

1. The Scriptures alone have final authority for faith and practice,
2. Salvation comes by faith alone and
3. The priesthood of every believer.

Though promoted 500 years ago, that third aspect of truth was never fully actualized. Every believer is called to be a priest and minister, but for the last 1800 years, the Church has been led primarily by pastors—individuals who care for and shepherd the flock. In many ways this has worked well, but Scripture declares the Church is built on the foundation of the *apostles and prophets*. This leads us to ask an important question:

What is the difference between a pastor-led church and an apostle-led church?

The simple answer is that the impulse of a pastor is to gather, keep and care, while the impulse of an apostle is to gather, train and send. What does this mean for us?

Times are changing.

Ultimately, we have a goal—the Great Commission. All authority has been given to Christ because of what He accomplished through His death, burial and resurrection. That authority was transferred to us so we could make disciples out of every nation, tribe and tongue around the world. We can go beyond discipling individuals to discipling whole people groups, because Jesus wants to be powerfully manifested on the earth. He prayed in Matthew 6:

"Your kingdom come.
Your will be done
On earth as it is in heaven."

That is our commission as sons and daughters of God, and it requires seeing the role of the Church afresh, in a different way. When Jesus first used the Greek word *ecclesia,* or *church,* it was a secular word that meant "called out ones." It referred specifically to the elders who were called from the village to sit at the gates and preside on behalf of the community; they legislated righteousness and justice to serve the whole village. That means the Church has a greater role than simply being a "holding tank" for saved souls until they go to Heaven. Instead, it exists to be a place of training and sending, so we can go out in the name, power and wisdom of Jesus to bring transformation to the world around us, leading people into a living relationship with the living God. That is the apostolic model—to gather, train and send for maximum impact in the world.

As we talk about the apostolic, it is not our intent to diminish the value of the pastoral gift. The pastoral gift is essential to the well-being of God's people and should never be seen as secondary. At the same time, we want to reinforce the importance of the apostolic and highlight where we feel God is leading His Church in this season, which means we need to differentiate between the two gifts and talk about their unique aspects.

How Do We Grow More Apostolic?

Right now, the Church at large recognizes only three gifts: the pastor, the evangelist and the teacher. While those three are widely promoted throughout the Body of Christ, in general we have neglected the other two gifts—the apostle and prophet—because they are "dangerous." We know what it's like when they are misused, and so we marginalize them for safety. But all five of these gifts were given at the same time, for the same purpose: that we grow up into Him who is the head of all things. The apostle Paul put it like this:

Speaking the truth in love, [we are to] grow up in all things into Him who is the head—Christ—from whom the whole body, joined and knit together by what every joint supplies, according to the effective working by which every part does its share, causes growth of the body for the edifying of itself in love.
— *Ephesians 4:15-16*

At Pastor's Coach, we strongly believe that when Jesus ascended, the gifts He gave to the Body of Christ were given to equip us in the different aspects of His ministry. These gifts are not about titles and positions; they are *primarily* about function and fruit.

As these gifts function in the Body of Christ, the whole body is edified according to the specific aspects of the ministry of Jesus, and the health we receive will produce the outcome of Ephesians 4:16.

With that understanding, let's take a look at leadership and how you can fill a region with churches that are ready to be a part of the greatest harvest the world has ever seen.

The Premise of Leadership

Many different theories exist to help churches grow, but the one that stands the test of biblical scrutiny is church growth through leadership development.

To give you an example, San Francisco is an extremely difficult mission field. Many church plants arrive in the Bay Area with lots of money, a good leader, a great mail campaign and creative advertisements, and in the beginning, several of them see good fruit. Yet their long-term impact ends up being low.

Why?

In most cases, they fail to develop the leadership core needed to sustain a long-term move of God.

In the Gospels, Jesus had a specific strategy for building leaders, and we call it *concentricity* at Pastor's Coach. First, He called 12 men to walk with Him and be trained to carry His ministry into the future. As He worked with those 12, He focused His attention a bit more on three core leaders: Peter, James and John. In addition to the 12, He developed a wider team of 70 others and expanded from there. Jesus developed concentric levels of leaders around Him, like the rings of a bulls-eye. He had His core team and each subsequent ring of leadership built outward from the center point.

In the classic book *The Master Plan of Evangelism* (Fleming H. Revell Co: 1986), Robert E. Coleman wrote that when Jesus set out to bring transformation to the earth, He had no other plan to extend the Kingdom than to make disciples and then send those disciples out to make other disciples. That was Plan A. There was no Plan B. His way of transforming the world was to transform 12 individuals, whom He sent out to transform others.

What does this mean for us? The average church in America has about 60 people. The primary reason for this is that a single person can care for only about 60 others without assistance. In order to break this barrier, the pastor needs to learn how to lead through leaders, a transition that is much more challenging than one might think. It requires a complete change in ministry culture and practice.

Every leader has a serious choice to make: You can *pastor people* or you can *lead leaders*. Jesus chose to lead leaders, and those people went out and radically changed the world.

Quintessential Leadership: A Picture of Jesus on Earth

As you read this, you are surrounded by a divine concept that influences your everyday interactions, how you think, who you are as an individual and your purpose and destiny. You can see this concept throughout Scripture—it is the *unity and diversity of God.*

God made us to reflect His manifold wisdom (Ephesians 3:10). All of us are unique and different, exotic and noteworthy—we all reflect Him in some manner. And all of us can find ourselves in the list of ascension gifts described in Ephesians 4:11-13, because these are aspects of who Jesus is:

He Himself gave some to be apostles, some prophets, some evangelists, and some pastors and teachers, for the equipping of the saints for the work of ministry, for the edifying of the body of Christ, till we all come to the unity of the faith and of the knowledge of the Son of God, to a perfect man, to the measure of the stature of the fullness of Christ.

Jesus is the Apostle and High Priest of our faith (Hebrews 3:1). He is the Great Prophet (Deuteronomy 18:15) and the good Shepherd or pastor (John 10:11). He is the Teacher (Matthew 22:36) and the One sent from Heaven with good news, which makes Him the evangelist (Isaiah 61:1). When He gave us these gifts, He was essentially *dividing* Himself and giving different members of His body different pieces or aspects of His own ministry. As reflections of Jesus, these gifts are the "substance" of who He is in His interactions with others.

**These gifts are the essence of the very
nature of Jesus, and when they work
together, they create a full picture of who He is.**

None of us are able to contain the fullness of Jesus alone, so He created *diversity* to dispense His gifting into various members across the Body of Christ. It is as if the Church is a prism, and as the white light of Jesus shines into us, it refracts into five primary "colors" and a myriad of blended combinations. He made each of us different, and yet we all look like Him.

The Body of Christ has many members but is one body under one head: Jesus. It takes all five gifts to create a complete picture of Jesus in a local church or ministry. As leaders, it is important for us to think in terms of promoting these aspects of ministry because they are the primary framework for how a church is to function.

Many people refer to the Ephesians 4 framework as the fivefold ministry, but at Pastor's Coach we prefer the term *quintessential leadership*. One of our favorite words, *quintessential* is based on an understanding of ancient Persian and Greek culture. They taught on the four elements of the earth: earth, air, water and fire. But they also theorized that a fifth element bound the rest together. People have quantified the fifth element in different ways, but it was generally considered to be spirit, ether or love. When all five elements came together, they could produce an incredible synergy. In the Kingdom of God, the "fifth element" would be the apostolic, because nothing produces growth and Kingdom expansion like the apostolic gift.

Let's look at each of the five "elements" of Christ a little more closely and see how they apply to the new reformation of the Church.

Apostolic

The literal meaning of *apostle* is "sent one," or someone who is commissioned as a fully authorized representative of the sender. When we look at this definition through the lens of Ephesians 4, an apostle becomes "a sent one who sends." The apostle trains and sends new leaders and ministers and oversees leadership development, mobilizing, pioneering, missions, etc.

Prophetic

Prophetic means to speak on behalf of another. It includes our ability to connect with God, hear clearly what God is saying and express the words of God in all we do and say. The prophetic involves worship, intercession and the public use of spiritual gifts, all of them based and enveloped in the truth that God wants to indwell His people. The prophetic gifting allows for that indwelling to happen. It facilitates God's presence and power in His people, who want to know Him and hear His voice.

Evangelistic

The gospel is good news, and evangelism is the proclamation of the gospel in word and deed. It involves the presentation of truth and apologetics; serving the poor; and anything else that clearly proclaims and demonstrates the good news of the Kingdom of God, including demonstrations of God's supernatural power to convict, heal and deliver those who come to Him.

Pastoral

At the heart of every pastor is the cultivation of caring community—community that responds in counsel, love and true support for its people. Like an experienced shepherd, the pastor helps feed the people, shelters them as they grow, provides for them and protects them from harm.

Teaching

Teachers are entrusted with the Word of God at a special level. It isn't the truth we hear that makes us free; it is the truth that confronts falsehood inside us—truth that deals with the lies and evicts them from our hearts. This delivery of truth requires an anointed teacher who can bring God's truth to the human heart. Such deliveries occur one-on-one through personal discipleship, in small groups and in large group gatherings.

Those are the five elements of Jesus and His ministry on the earth in their basic forms. This is what His ministry looks like on the earth. As a pastor, it is possible to structure your church in such a way that every group in your church can incorporate each of these elements, providing the full spectrum of Jesus' ministry to every person they touch. This means that each leadership team, small group and ministry group would have an evangelistic emphasis, a community-building emphasis, a teaching and discipleship emphasis, a prophetic emphasis and an apostolic emphasis.

We built the first five themes of the *Pastor's Coach Assessment: Church Health Assessment (C.H.A.)* around the five aspects of Christ, so we'll look at ways you can purposefully grow in these different elements in your church. These segments are designed to jumpstart you—they will help you think in new ways about your church's growth, health and impact. They will fuel the fire within you to connect with God, connect with others and lead people forward in God's purposes.

One Plan to Change the World

As we talked about, Jesus had one plan for changing the world: Disciple people who would disciple nations. So the first function of every job description in a church should be to recruit and raise up its replacement (for the purpose of replicating the group and starting new groups). Your first job as a leader is to raise up the next leader. In this way the church grows, and you grow, and the life of God fills your city and region.

As much as possible, build leadership development into every branch of your church.

As John Wimber, founder of the Vineyard Movement, said, "I never pay someone to do a job. I only pay those who can get others to do a job." Help your leaders learn to *identify*, *recruit*, *train*, *deploy*, *monitor* and *nurture* new leaders as their first priority. In the process, your whole church becomes an incubator for leadership.

You have chosen to embark on a journey of bringing health to the local church. Thank you for joining us as we discuss what it means to be a thriving church, one that is powerfully bringing transformation and impact to the region.

— Dr. Michael Brodeur
CEO and founder,
www.PastorsCoach.com
www.DestinyFinder.com

Theme 1
Apostolic Purpose

**We value God's blueprint for building the Church
and transforming the world.**

This theme includes:

- God's heart for the apostolic (1 Corinthians 3:10; Ephesians 2:20)
- Our vision is clearly stated and is understood by all our members.
- We have clarified our values and cultivated a strong Kingdom culture.
- Our members embrace their responsibility to serve God and others.
- Multiplication of new ministry is built into everything we do.
- We effectively train and release emerging apostolic leaders.

An Introduction to the Apostolic Gift

*Now, therefore, you are no longer strangers and foreigners, but fellow
citizens with the saints and members of the household of God, having
been built on the foundation of the apostles and prophets, Jesus Christ
Himself being the chief cornerstone.*
— Ephesians 2:19-20

It is interesting that Jesus' plan to change the world began the same way
creation did. Adam and Eve were given a mandate to "be fruitful and
multiply. Fill the earth and subdue it." In response, they gave birth to
children, who gave birth to children, and humanity went on to fill the earth
and steward the planet on God's behalf.

In our generation, we have a mandate of discipleship, which is similar to the
mandate found in Genesis 1. Instead of natural, biological family, we see
spiritual family and spiritual transformation as people are born again by the
Spirit of God. These people are then trained up in "households" of local
church expression and empowered to bear fruit. They are sent out to have

sons and daughters of their own in the various spheres of society to which God has called them. That is the essence of the apostolic calling.

> **In its purest definition, the purpose of the**
> **apostolic gifting is "a sent one who sends."**
> **It is a spiritual parent who raises up sons**
> **and daughters according to God's design**
> **and sends them out to fulfill their destinies.**

Despite our hesitation to use it today, the word *apostle* is used much more frequently in Scripture than the word *pastor*. It is also used about many more individuals. In the New Testament, more than 25 people are listed as apostles, and one of them is a woman. Somehow we have made the mistake of "mystifying" the gift and, in some ways, setting it beyond our reach. In so doing, we have created an imbalance in the intent and heart of Scripture.

What is God's heart concerning the apostolic gift? Let's take a look.

The Apostolic Gift

Most of us think of apostles as people who plant churches, heal the sick and so forth, and yes, apostles are called to function in the full authority of Jesus. However, the emphasis in Ephesians 4 is not so much on the *function* of an apostle but on the apostle's role as an *equipper*.

> **In other words, the apostle is meant**
> **to impart her gift to the larger group.**

We could think of the apostle as a spiritual architect who sees a heavenly blueprint and is able to marshal the forces, resources and human talents necessary to build what he sees. As Paul describes in 1 Corinthians 3:10, apostles are master builders who release other people to contribute to the building according to their unique gifts and callings in Christ. Apostles lay foundations and establish the "footprint" of what the Body of Christ is supposed to look like. People with apostolic callings are also consistently aware of the urgency of the gospel, and they are eager to mobilize God's people to complete His mission on earth.

As we look at the apostolic gift, we need to remember that it expresses itself in different models in different people. We could think of them as different apostolic "flavors." Peter was different than Paul. Paul was different than Barnabas. The apostolic calling is not a one-size-fits-all calling. Instead, there are *prophetic* apostles, *pastoral* apostles, *teaching* apostles and so forth—these are people who have true apostolic callings but express them with a different style and flavor than an apostolic leader in a different stream.

Apostles and Prophets

The role of apostle is often mentioned alongside the role of prophet. In a sense, these two gifts are mutually interdependent. Like a husband-and-wife team raising a family, the different elements of Christ that are represented in these two gifts work together along with the other three gifts of Ephesians 4:11 to create a solid foundation on which the Church can thrive. Although we have examples in Scripture of the gifts working apart from one another, we also have the testimony of Acts 15, where Paul and Barnabas (apostles) proclaimed the council's decision, and Judas and Silas (prophets) confirmed it.

In summary, these gifts need one another. The apostle without a prophet is in danger of building a "factory" (church structures without the Spirit), while the prophet without an apostle will eventually build a "fantasy" (subjective impressions without healthy structure).

What If You're Not Apostolic?

Not every senior leader is called to be an apostle or will function with apostolic leadership as his or her primary gift. But that doesn't need to hinder the leader from being apostolic.

Here's how it works. The five aspects of Christ (the quintessential or fivefold leadership gifts) were given to equip the Church for the work of the ministry. Sometimes we make the mistake of putting the individuals who function in these gifts up on a pedestal, and we forget that Ephesians 4 is all about empowering *others* into fruitful ministry. Because these ministry gifts are about equipping the body, all of us are able to draw from these leaders the resources we need to fulfill our roles more effectively. In other words, even if we are not called to be apostles, we can still draw from apostolic leaders a measure of "apostolic grace" that empowers us to be more apostolic than we would be otherwise.

Let's say Steve is a pastor with a pastor's wiring. He is a connector and a shepherd who is not heavily gifted in the apostolic. However, he wants to grow in this area, so he spends a lot of time reading apostolic biographies, meeting with apostolic leaders and attending conferences where apostolic leaders are speaking. Every time he is around someone who is thinking and acting in an apostolic fashion, it impacts him and enhances his ability to function more apostolically.

**Steve doesn't have to be called
as an apostle to be apostolic.**

He can still be equipped by apostolic leaders. We need to be exposed to every aspect of Christ so we can be enhanced in all His aspects.

As another example, you have the ability to appropriate and apply what you are reading right now. Much of what we are teaching you through Pastor's Coach is apostolic in nature. You may not be inherently wired to think or act in an apostolic way, but your exposure to this material and your willingness to learn can help you be more apostolic than you would be naturally.

The Current Apostolic Reformation

The apostolic gift has functioned in every generation since the time of Jesus. Most apostles were called pastors, reverends or something similar, but we can see their apostolic gifting in how they built strong, reproducing churches. Some apostles were missionaries who went out and laid a foundation where no other foundation existed, and some expressed themselves in other unique ways. We can see the apostolic gift in every generation—we just sometimes called it different names.

If you have any doubts about the ongoing existence of apostles in our generation, a simple study of Ephesians 4:7-16 will shed some light. All five gifts were given at the same time (the ascension of Jesus), for the same purpose (the equipping of the saints for ministry) and until the same time (until all of us together become a unified, perfect body that fully represents

Jesus). Do you think we've reached that goal? Clearly, we still have a long ways to go. You could also think about it like this: If apostles and prophets have passed away, it must be that teachers and pastors have passed away as well.

Interestingly, the word *pastor* is used only once in Scripture as a noun to describe anyone other than Jesus. That one time occurs in the Ephesians 4 passage we've been discussing. Yet the word *apostle* is used more than a hundred times in the New Testament and refers to more than two-dozen different individuals.

> **If the role of pastor still exists, the role of apostle must still exist as well.**

As we talked about earlier, the Church has diminished the apostolic gift. This occurred partly out of a misguided respect for the original apostles and partly because we didn't know how to handle the implied authority apostles carry. It is time to brush away the cobwebs and refocus, because apostolic leadership is the next major transition coming to the Body of Christ. Some call what God is doing right now the *new apostolic reformation*, a phrase originally coined by Peter Wagner in his book *Church Quake! The Explosive Power of the New Apostolic Reformation* (Regal: 1999). Although some people criticize the way his insights have been applied, we believe the basic concepts are worthy of careful consideration.

In summary, the Body of Christ is in a massive shift that, frankly, is going to change the world. We are moving away from being a pastor-led Church to an apostle-led Church. Pastors are geared to protect the flock, while apostles are geared to extend the Kingdom. Pastors without apostles can find themselves creating consumer-driven spectators who depend on others to feed and care for them. Apostles, on the other hand, will create empowered disciples who are increasingly equipped to bring the Kingdom of Heaven into all areas and aspects of life.

But remember, even though the Body of Christ is in a massive transition from pastoral to apostolic, we have no desire to minimize the importance of the pastoral role. That is not our heart at all. The pastoral gift is absolutely essential for every healthy church to have thriving community and relationship between its members. According to 1 Corinthians 12:28, primary leadership should be apostolic, but we need both gifts—the apostle and the pastor—to build a flourishing church.

1.1
Apostolic Vision

**Focal point: Our vision is clearly stated and
is understood by all our members.**

This focal point includes:

- Discover God's vision for your church and make it known to them.
- Be aligned with a movement and apostolic oversight.
- Understand the Church's overall vision.

  *Where there is no revelation [that is, vision], the people cast off
  restraint.*
  — Proverbs 29:18

At the moment of his salvation, the apostle Paul received what he called a "heavenly vision" (Acts 26:19). One encounter with God, and the course of his life changed forever. His ministry shifted the world—and it all began when Jesus encountered him on the road to Damascus.

Years later, Paul described himself as a *master builder*, which essentially is a general contractor who has primary responsibility for the blueprint of Heaven. Let's look at a few elements that are important to consider when you're seeking God's blueprint for your church:

1. Discover God's vision for your church and make it known to them.

What births apostolic vision within a church leader? Consider the following components:

- Fasting and prayer
- Seeking the Lord
- Listening to His voice
- Paying attention to prophetic dreams, visions and other encounters

The leader is responsible to communicate vision to the congregation, letting them know, "This is where we are going as a church. This is what you can expect. This is what you can be excited about and be a part of."

One true apostolic test is if you can take a beautiful, inspiring vision and create strategies and structures (home groups, ministry teams, children ministry, etc.) to make it reality. What steps does your church need to take to see the blueprint become a real "building," with life and form off the page? Know how to set goals, priorities and objectives and be able to mobilize your team to fulfill these things. An apostolic leader also needs to be a great implementer—or at least know how to recruit and partner with great implementers.

2. Be aligned with a movement and apostolic oversight.

At Pastor's Coach, we recommend that every church have some form of outside apostolic oversight from a specific denomination or movement. If this isn't an option for whatever reason, the church can enlist a few proven apostolic overseers to guide them and help them troubleshoot any problems that arise.

Here are two reasons alignment is incredibly important for any church:

- As a leader, your personal alignment with an apostolic "parent" will empower those you lead to be more aligned with you.
- Alignment inspires "tribal vision," which gives your church a larger picture of where you are going. Being joined to a larger family or "tribe" of churches gives your local vision greater context.

3. Understand the Church's overall vision.

The ultimate vision of the Body of Christ is to reach the unreached with the gospel, transforming lives, spheres and regions in the name of Jesus. The ultimate apostolic vision—the vision that encompasses all other visions—is releasing the Kingdom of Heaven in such a way that every other kingdom is brought low.

Therefore, the apostolic urgency is to mobilize as many believers as possible and help them understand their unique gifts, callings and authority in Christ. As they are empowered, they are released to impact the spheres God called them to influence, so the Kingdom of Heaven can continue to advance on individual and societal levels.

1.2
Apostolic Culture

Focal point: We have clarified our values and cultivated a strong Kingdom culture.

This focal point includes:

- Culture is to community what habit is to an individual.
- Culture is based in shared values, priorities and practices that unite us.
- Personify the culture and infuse it into your leadership team.
- Bring the culture to your congregation through teaching and modeling.

> *"Heaven is My throne,*
> *And earth is My footstool.*
> *Where is the house that you will build Me?*
> *And where is the place of My rest?"*
> — *Isaiah 66:1*

Culture is like the banks of a river. If there are no riverbanks, the river becomes a marsh, but where the banks are strong and stable, they channel the river's flow, taking it where it needs to go. Culture channels the flow of community to its maximum impact and value in the world around us.

Note: *In an effort to provide information about culture and how to build culture in your church, portions of the following information are repeated throughout our results.*

John Wimber, founder of the Vineyard Movement and a leader in the realm of church growth, was convinced that the healthiest churches were grown from the inside out. You can do this by determining what you as a church really care about. What are your values—the things that drive you? Not the things you *want* to care about, but the things you have proven you care about again and again?

Culture is the shared values, priorities and practices, along with the traditions, symbols and expressions, that unite a community and connect that community to its past, present and future. Your culture reveals who you are as a church. As you clarify your values, you establish your priorities—things that are more or less important for the allocation of your time, energy and resources. Then out of your priorities, your everyday practices emerge. All of these work to establish the apostolic *culture* of your church.

Culture is to community what habit and discipline are to an individual. Culture takes time to build, but once it is built, it has an amazing power to steer large groups. If we fail to build strong culture that is intentional, we will pay the price of an accidental, potentially conflicting culture that will have to be continuously monitored. But if we build healthy, strong, cohesive culture at the beginning of the process, we will birth a movement that doesn't necessarily need to be managed at the same micro level.

How to Build Apostolic Culture in Your Church

Simply put, apostolic culture focuses on developing people and organizations to be the best they can be in order to put together a true representation of God on earth.

Culture is best built from the inside out—first in the leader, then in the team and finally on the public level. Let's look at each of these steps more closely.

1. As a leader, personify the culture yourself.

Culture reflects the senior leader's lifestyle and the core community of the leadership team. Therefore, the first step in cultivating apostolic culture is for you, as a primary leader, to look at your own values and priorities. How are you carrying this culture into your personal family? Are you thinking about your people developmentally? Are you taking the time to work with them? Is the desire to develop people into the fullness of Christ integrated into your values, priorities and practices as a leader?

2. Infuse that culture into your primary team.

Give your core team a vision and infuse them with the values and priorities that will help them grow apostolic culture throughout the congregation.

With anything you want to cultivate within your church, begin in your leadership team. If you want your church to embrace evangelism, for example, you will need to take time to evangelize as a leadership team and celebrate evangelism in your core team in such a way that it affects the entire church. The same with pastoral care. If you want your church to embrace connection, community, small groups and so forth, celebrate and promote these things in your team of leaders.

Remember, the primary responsibility of every leader is to replicate herself in someone else. An apostolic culture will always gather, train and send out, so be prepared for growth in your church groups! Also, be open to adjustments in your leadership team and help them reach the goals for which God designed them.

3. Bring the culture to your congregation through teaching and modeling.

Begin to instill culture in your congregation through personal interaction, public preaching, testimonies and ongoing celebration of cultural successes.

An apostolic culture thrives when its individual members discover who they are in Christ and are empowered and equipped to impact the world around them, both in the church and outside it. They do this as they develop and cultivate their gifts and callings in Jesus.

1.3
Apostolic Lifestyle

**Focal point: Our members embrace their responsibility
to serve God and others.**

This focal point includes:

- Give your people a vision for apostolic community.
- Understand where your church is in the growth process.
- Celebrate apostolic leadership wherever you find it.

> *"I will put My law in their minds, and write it on their hearts; and I
> will be their God, and they shall be My people."*
> — *Jeremiah 31:33*

As an apostolic lifestyle becomes more and more important to your church, a set of practices begins to emerge that reflects the things your church does naturally. You don't do them because you are *told* to do them or because you have a program set up that helps you do them. Instead, you do them automatically because you love Jesus, His Word and His purposes, and these things are deeply entrenched in your heart as a community. The values you embraced have become a way of life for you.

Let's look at some hands-on, practical ways you can build an apostolic lifestyle in your church:

1. Give your people a vision for apostolic community.

An apostolic lifestyle begins when we realize why we are here. We know we are here for a purpose, and we want to please the Lord, not ourselves. The Church's overall goal is the Great Commission, and when we really understand the following verses, our desire for a true apostolic lifestyle will grow:

"Go therefore and make disciples of all the nations, baptizing them in the name of the Father and of the Son and of the Holy Spirit, teaching them to observe all things that I have commanded you; and lo, I am with you always, even to the end of the age."
— *Matthew 28:19-20*

That is the first step in building an apostolic lifestyle—making sure the Great Commission has preeminence in everything you do.

2. Understand where your church is in the growth process.

Your church's lifestyle revolves around its values and priorities. How would you answer the following questions?

- What does your church value? How does the church prioritize those values?
- Does your church value serving God and people?
- Look at how your church members manage their money, spend their time and allocate their talents. Generally speaking, are people giving God their best and honoring Him with their lifestyle choices?
- Is your church's movement and growth balanced and sustainable over the long haul?

When it comes to how you manage your time, energy, money and resources, most of the challenges will be about your *ecosystem*. Certain factors interface with each other to create balance in our lives. If that balance begins to lean toward our own interests, we will find ourselves getting sucked down a path toward selfishness. But when we realize what's happening, we can start adjusting our choices and priorities, so relationship with Jesus again becomes our focal point.

To put it bluntly, most problems in our lives come about because we aren't fully giving our hearts to Jesus. That might sound a little harsh, but it's true. Matthew 6:33 says that if we seek first God's righteousness and the Kingdom of Heaven, everything else is added to us. That is a point of faith we need to exercise, realizing, *Wait a minute. If I put anything above God, it's going to mess up my life, but if I put God and His purposes first, He will make sure I live a balanced, full, fruitful, fun life. Why? Because He wants the best for me.*

3. Celebrate apostolic leadership wherever you find it.

Preach on the subject of building an apostolic lifestyle. Celebrate actual apostles (people who are known to be apostolic leaders), as well as the members of your church who are moving in apostolic ways by starting ministries, small businesses, organizations, non-profits, etc. As leaders, we have an amazing opportunity to mirror the heart of Jesus as we encourage those around us to go forth and build.

1.4
Apostolic Structures

**Focal point: Multiplication of new ministry
is built into all we do.**

This focal point includes:

- New ministries serve a similar function as new churches.
- Articulate your vision and submit it for counsel.
- Share the vision and build a team.
- Launch the ministry and make adjustments as you go.

> *Therefore, holy brethren, partakers of the heavenly calling, consider the
> Apostle and High Priest of our confession, Christ Jesus.*
> — *Hebrews 3:1*

Ministries are like vehicles. They work well for a time and then you trade
them in for a newer model. You don't expect a car to last forever, and it costs
a lot of money if you try to make it last forever!

Always be open to new ministries in your church, because they serve a similar
function as new churches—church plants have proven to be the most
effective tool for extending the Kingdom. Here's why:

- They employ maximum momentum with a fresh start and vision,
  which draws people.
- They also provide members with opportunities for service, input and
  exciting connections with new people who are looking for a church.
- More people are saved, more leaders are developed, more ministries
  are pioneered and more Kingdom impact is made in church plants
  than in any other expression of the Kingdom.

How to Start a New Ministry in Your Church

The key for apostolic success is the church leader's openness to start new ministries.

Here's a basic overview for starting a new ministry: To start a ministry, identify a leader who can take your apostolic vision and practices and turn them into a structure such as a home group, ministry group, etc. Your vision is what you're called to do, and your practices are what you actually do on a daily basis. When your vision and practices combine beneath the strength of a leader, that leader can create something that transforms your church and brings Heaven to earth in your region.

Let's look a little more closely at how to build a ministry:

1. Articulate your vision and submit it for counsel.

Every ministry begins with a blueprint of what it is supposed to become. In other words, you begin with the end in mind. Ask yourself, "What is my goal? What is my purpose in building this ministry?" Clarify your vision with Scripture, and be able to articulate the outcome you intend to achieve.

2. Share the vision and build a team.

A healthy team is absolutely essential for a successful ministry. This requires boldness on your part because you'll need to share your vision with those you believe God has called to walk with you and invite them into the building process. As you build your team, try to identify each person's gifts and callings and assign responsibilities appropriately. The profiling tool we offer at www.DestinyFinder.com could help you better understand and build your team.

3. Launch the ministry and make adjustments as you go.

Set a date for your first event and do the necessary publicity, invitations, social networking, etc. After the event, take time to evaluate with your team. What worked? What didn't work? How can you improve? Which team members are committed for the long haul? Also, try to get feedback from those who came to the event. These evaluations are incredibly helpful as you move forward.

1.5
Apostolic Leadership

**Focal point: We effectively train and release
emerging apostolic leaders.**

This focal point includes:

- The local church exists primarily to be a leadership incubator (Matthew 28:18-20).
- Identify emerging apostolic leaders and mentor them into their roles.
- As people develop in their destinies, they grow into leadership.
- The more you can identify new apostolic leaders and pour into them, the more fruitful your ministry will be as a church and the more impactful you will be overall.

   "Therefore whoever hears these sayings of Mine, and does them, I will liken him to a wise man who built his house on the rock: and the rain descended, the floods came, and the winds blew and beat on that house; and it did not fall, for it was founded on the rock."
   — Matthew 7:24-25

The local church is meant to be a leadership incubator (Matthew 28:18-20). The power of apostolic ministry in your church depends on your ability, as a primary leader, to identify emerging apostolic leaders and mentor them into their roles. As they pioneer new ministries, they raise up the next generation of apostolic leaders and complete the cycle: Spiritual children mature into spiritual adults, who produce more spiritual children.

Do you know who in your congregation has an apostolic calling? You could use a gift assessment tool like the one we offer at www.DestinyFinder.com to help identify the gifts and callings of individuals in your church.

Keep your eyes open for a number of apostolic traits:

- Apostles tend to see the big picture.

- They have a sense of the overall mission of Jesus.
- They appreciate each of the gifts of the Spirit and see how they can function together for maximum impact.
- They tend to be strategic thinkers and understand the immense value of operating in God's presence and power.
- They know how to build; they can take a vision and make it reality.
- They easily gather people and call out the best in them.

The more you identify those in your church who are apostolically oriented and begin to pour into them, the more fruitful your ministry will be as a church and the more impactful you will be overall.

Raising Up Leaders

At Pastor's Coach, we have five steps to leading leaders. We adapted this list from John Wimber's teaching on development.

1. Identify

Begin by thinking about what your team needs. What are your strengths as a team and what are your weaknesses? Do you need a great administrator? Do you need an apostolic father? Identify what you need and ask God to bring that specific gift to you. Look at the people around you and ask God who He is leading to work with you.

2. Recruit

Spend time with the people God is highlighting to you. Feel them out to see if they share your vision and values. Start inviting them to do things with you, and seek to hear from God for them in order to bless and build them up.

Actual recruiting looks like going to the person and saying, "I've been praying, and now that I know you better, I really think you have the gift mix I need. Would you please pray about walking with me in what I'm about to do?" Recruit them into what you are building.

3. Train

Everyone you are leading needs to be trained in what you are doing. Spend time with your people; share your vision, values and goals with them; and train them in the specific functions you are asking them to carry out.

4. Deploy

Deployment is the process of turning loose those you trained to lead. Don't give them meaningless tasks that don't allow them to be leaders; instead, trust them to lead in your absence and do what you would do in that situation. They should have real responsibilities as well as your trust.

**A worker is someone who serves
in the presence of her leader,
but a *leader* is one who serves in the absence of her leader.**

5. Support: Monitor and Nurture

After you deploy the leaders under you, *monitor* their activity in a way that builds them up and helps them go even further. Make sure the quality of what they are doing matches your criteria, while you keep encouraging and blessing them.

Nurturing is essentially pastoral care. Most burnout occurs when monitoring and nurturing haven't happened or happened poorly. If you turn people loose with a job to do but you never check in with them, they could be out there floundering, needing parenting and a loving, steady hand to lead them forward. Love them. Keep leading them. Allow them to grow.

If you walk out these five steps with your leaders, you will have an ever-multiplying leadership team that will carry your pastoral care to a growing congregation.

Theme 1: Apostolic Purpose

Theme 2
Prophetic Purpose

**We value God's presence and power and welcome
God to move in our midst.**

This theme includes:

- The supernatural has been a part of every Kingdom expansion in history.
- Intercession, prayer and hearing from God are priorities in everything we do.
- We commit time, energy and resource to pursuing God's presence.
- We cultivate an environment where people encounter God.
- The gifts and manifestations of the Holy Spirit are abundant in our ministries.
- We effectively train, release and mentor new prophetic leaders.

An Introduction to the Prophetic Gift

Whom have I in heaven but You?
And there is none upon earth that I desire besides You.
— Psalm 73:25

Then he said to Him, "If Your Presence does not go with us, do not bring us up from here."
— Exodus 33:15

Without the presence and power of God, Christianity is just another religion.

In Acts 2 Peter quotes one of the most significant prophecies ever given about the New Covenant Jesus inaugurated in His death, burial and resurrection: "I will pour out of My Spirit on all flesh; your sons and your daughters shall prophesy." As followers of Jesus, we are born again and indwelt by the Spirit of the Living God, and therefore we are a prophetic people. We read in the New Testament about those who were uniquely gifted as prophets, and that gift was never taken away. Prophets have always lived among us.

In the last 2000 years, the Church has never failed to experience some move of God's Spirit. Prophecy occurs repeatedly in the book of Acts, and we can find incredible stories that occurred after the end of Acts as well. Whether you are studying the early Church in the first and second centuries; St. Patrick and the Irish monasteries in the fourth century; the Benedictine and Franciscan periods of the Catholic Church; or the Protestant movements, revivals and the Great Awakenings—you will find signs, wonders and other kinds of amazing spiritual expressions. Throughout history we can find *many* examples of supernatural things. Prophecies were given to foretell, correct and bring God's perspective in given seasons.

The prophetic dimensions of the Holy Spirit came into better focus at the turn of the last century, beginning with the Welsh Revival in 1904. That revival was later echoed on Azusa Street in the United States, and in the last 100 years, the Pentecostal revival has grown to become the largest, most impactful expression of Kingdom reality ever to occur.

Right now, it is estimated that several hundred *million* charismatic and Pentecostal believers around the world understand the value of revelation and God's presence and power. Pentecostalism was the first "wave" of a deep, ongoing prophetic reformation. The second wave was the charismatic renewal in the 1960s and the third wave came in the 1980s, bringing a fresh understanding of the Holy Spirit's work that resulted in worldwide movements (such as the Vineyard Movement and the Toronto Movement).

In this moment, God is doing incredible things around the earth. People are hearing His voice and experiencing the prophetic realm in life-changing ways.

Different Levels of Prophetic Gifting

Moses wished that all God's people were prophets (Numbers 11:29). As we fast forward to the coming of Christ and the new covenant, that prayer is fulfilled:

> *"I will pour out of My Spirit on all flesh;*

Your sons and your daughters shall prophesy,
Your young men shall see visions,
Your old men shall dream dreams.'"
— Acts 2:17

The new covenant reality is that every single person who is filled with the Spirit is prophetic by nature. Traditionally, there are three "levels" of prophetic gifting commonly identified:

1. the gift of prophecy,
2. the ministry of prophecy and
3. the office of a prophet.

All of us have the basic ability to prophesy. We can hear God's voice and be led by His Spirit. Even if we don't consider ourselves "prophetic," we can expand our ability to hear His voice by studying the prophetic, learning *how* to hear Him and being around prophetic people.

Not every church leader is called
to be a prophet or will function with
prophetic leadership as his primary
gift. But that doesn't need to hinder
the leader from being prophetic.

As we talked about, the quintessential leadership gifts (the fivefold gifts) were given to equip the Church for the work of the ministry. This means that we are able to draw from fivefold leaders the resources we need to fulfill our roles more effectively. Even if we are not called to be prophets, we can still pull from prophetic leaders a measure of "prophetic grace" that empowers us to be more prophetic than we would be otherwise.

We need to be exposed to every aspect
of Christ so we can be enhanced in all His aspects.

As another example, you have the ability to appropriate and apply what you are reading right now. You may not be inherently wired to think or act in a prophetic way, but your exposure to this material and your willingness to learn can help you be more prophetic than you would be naturally.

The second level of prophetic gifting is the ministry of prophecy, which is the consistent gift of prophecy functioning in an individual. The people around that person and the church he attends recognize he has a prophetic gift that is more visible than most.

The third level is those who are recognized in the actual *office* of prophet. These are the people whose gifts have been refined, proven and confirmed over a period of years. They are known as prophets, and their gift is recognizable—and endorsable—by the greater Body of Christ. The office of the prophet is reserved for those God has called to function in prophecy at a high level (Elijah is an example).

Those are the three levels of the prophetic gift working in the local Body of Christ. No matter where you fall within these three levels, you can expand your gift and learn to hear God's voice more clearly and frequently.

The Key to the Prophetic Gift

The prophetic gift prioritizes revelatory ability and hosting God's presence. As Christians who want to hear God's voice, we value the prophetic and desire to foster a prophetic reality in our midst—but how?

Many of us have experienced how overemphasizing the prophetic can be harmful to God's greater purposes. We've seen prophetic gifts used inappropriately in one way or another. Yet this gift is indispensable for the full measure of Christ to be manifested in the Church.

The prophetic gift needs to be coupled with other fivefold gifts so it provides strength to the body and can stay focused more easily.

It is helpful for prophets to work alongside teachers, for example, because the prophet tends to interpret Scripture from a more experiential, revelatory standpoint; prophets don't always focus on the intended meaning of the original author, while teachers research the nitty-gritty details and can tell you why something means what it means.

Prophets and pastors sometimes experience challenges because the prophet can have a pretty rigid idea of what "ought" to be. Most prophetic people are black and white in the way they perceive reality, whereas pastors tend to be more "gray" in their approach and focus more on process than destination. A similar situation exists between prophets and evangelists. Much of the time, prophets don't mind if the church is "crazy" with different manifestations of the Spirit, expressions of worship and chaotic dimensions, but the evangelist understands that these things don't always translate well to the new believer. So there can be tension between the gifts.

If we want to walk the prophetic road well, what is the key? It is to partner the prophetic and apostolic gifts (Ephesians 2:20). The prophet needs the apostle and the apostle needs the prophet in order for both to operate at their best.

The Prophet and the Apostle

The prophetic gift comes into right relationship with the body when it is paired with the apostolic gift. This "husband and wife" relationship is emphasized throughout Scripture. Even in the Old Testament, we can find foreshadowing apostolic and prophetic partnerships. David worked closely with a couple of prophets (Gad and Nathan), and during Israel's restoration period, Zerubbabel worked with Zechariah and Haggai. This kind of partnership is repeated in the New Testament as apostles and prophets worked together in the book of Acts (for example, the council in Acts 15 and Agabus using Paul's belt in Acts 21). The words *apostle* and *prophet* are used in unison in Ephesians 2-3.

Prophets and apostles understand their gifts best when they are working together in right relationship. Prophets are strong in revelation, while apostles are generally stronger in wisdom and application. This doesn't mean that prophets don't have wisdom or that apostles don't have revelation, but all of us have strengths God gave us to steward. The relationship between the prophet and apostle is a tangible manifestation of the spirit of wisdom and revelation (Isaiah 11:2).

Every apostolic leader needs to walk closely with prophetic leaders, and every prophetic leader needs to have apostolic alignment and covering in her life, according to the patterns laid out in Scripture. This apostolic/prophetic partnership is foundational to a healthy expression of Christ (Ephesians 2:20). The prophet without an apostle will tend to produce a realm of *fantasy* (subjective impressions without structure), while the apostle without the prophet will tend to produce a realm of *factory* (structures without the Spirit). We need both gifts operating together to produce true spiritual family.

2.1
Prophetic Vision

**Focal point: Intercession, prayer and hearing from God
are priorities in all we do.**

This focal point includes:

- Prophetic vision is all about God's presence.
- Every follower of Jesus is called to be prophetic.
- If you are born again and have the Spirit of God dwelling in you, you have entered a new prophetic dimension.
- Make the vision practical; model the vision and make it a priority to your staff and church.

> *You are my portion, O Lord;*
> *I have said that I would keep Your words.*
> *— Psalm 119:57*

Prophetic vision is, first of all, about God's presence. We are called to be people who foster the very presence of God in our congregations, learning how to favor and interact with His presence through worship, prayer, waiting on Him, soaking and biblical meditation.

Every follower of Jesus is called to be prophetic. Moses emphasized this in Numbers 11 when the Holy Spirit fell upon the 70—and then two other people as well. Joshua asked, "Should we stop them?"

"No," Moses replied. "I would that all God's people be prophets."

Moses got his wish in the New Testament when the Holy Spirit was poured out on all flesh (Acts 2). The result of Pentecost was that all God's people became prophetic.

In the Old Testament the Holy Spirit came upon only certain individuals, but in the New Covenant, if you are born again and have the Spirit of God dwelling in you, you have entered a new prophetic dimension.

How to Grow a Prophetic Vision in Your Church

1. Make the vision practical.

The vision for the presence needs to be practical, practiced and celebrated. *Practical* simply means that you teach on it regularly and reinforce its different aspects within your church. Try to give your congregation a picture of what a church filled with the Spirit looks like—it is a group of people who are baptized afresh in God's power. They interact in intimacy and love with Him and are filled with praise and joy because He is in their midst. They also interact with each other in love and honor, treasuring Christ in each person.

If you can encapsulate that vision—what a Spirit-filled church really looks like—you're on your way to instilling this vision in your congregation.

2. Model the vision.

Preach the vision of every church member being a prophetic conduit, and as a leader, *model* the vision on a daily basis. Are you walking in the prophetic? Are you cultivating and nurturing it? Are you learning to hear the voice of God better? Are you learning to host a conscious awareness of His presence throughout your day? Are you aware of the spiritual atmosphere around you? Are you learning to discern the different spirits around you? These are all elements of walking in the prophetic.

3. Make the prophetic vision a priority for your staff and church.

Be certain your staff know your vision for the prophetic, and be sure they are on the same page as you.

Also, strongly encourage everyone in your church to seek the Lord personally. Make pursuing God a priority, both individually and organizationally, and go after His presence as a group. You can do this through worship gatherings, prayer meetings and ministry to one another. Purposefully set aside time to meet with God and interact with Him, and celebrate when He shows up in powerful or unique ways. If you want more of Jesus and His presence in your midst, it is important to encourage testimonies of healings, miracles and encounters with God. Celebrate these things over and over again. People will emulate what you celebrate.

It's easy to celebrate well-known prophets (those in the actual office of prophet), but we also need to celebrate the "regular" members of the church who are moving in the prophetic with words of knowledge, words of wisdom, discerning of spirits and prophetic utterance. Remember that even if a prophetic word is inaccurate in the moment, we can still celebrate that the person took a risk. We will never grow in accuracy without mistakes being made from time to time.

If you honor God's presence, it will gradually increase in your midst, and the people you're leading will have a greater and greater experience of the presence and power of God.

2.2
Prophetic Culture

**Focal point: We commit time, energy and resources
to pursuing God's presence.**

This focal point includes:

- Culture is based in shared values, priorities and practices that unite us.
- Define your values, priorities and practices around God's presence.
- Personify the culture and infuse it into your leadership team.
- Make the prophetic a natural part of your church body.

> *Surely the Lord God does nothing,*
> *Unless He reveals His secret to His servants the prophets.*
> *— Amos 3:7*

The best way to increase your church's experience of God's presence and power is by building a prophetic culture. *Culture* is the shared values, priorities and practices, along with the traditions, symbols and expressions, that unite a community.

Building the right kind of culture is the first step in moving from vision to reality. Many of us have a strong vision of what we want to do and what we want to become, but vision alone will not get us to our goal. We need practical steps along the way. Culture takes time to build, but once it is built, it has an amazing power to steer large groups.

As a pastor, if you want to build a certain culture in your church, you have to begin to adjust your values—who you are as a church—at a fundamental level. These are some of the key values that undergird the prophetic:

- Intimacy (both with God and one another)
- Dependency on the Holy Spirit
- Integrity (which ensures the quality of the prophetic)

When values are combined with priorities (what has precedence in your daily life) and practices (what you actually do in your daily life), they become a cultural component. The three values listed above heighten our love and passion for the Lord and promote a culture of the supernatural and prophetic. They also give birth to the culture of honor, where we recognize the importance of each individual.

How to Build Prophetic Culture in Your Church

1. Define your values, priorities and practices around God's presence.

As you work to establish a prophetic culture in your church, think about these questions:

- How much time are you going to devote to worship, ministry and people who are being trained to minister to one another?
- How will you explain to visitors who you are and how you do what you do?
- What is the main emphasis of your budget?
- Where is most of your energy going?
- Does your family experience the prophetic at home?
- Do you as a leader go after God's power and presence personally? Everything you want to bring to your church has to be real inside of you first.

2. Incorporate the prophetic in your team.

How much time are you spending in your elder and staff meetings waiting on the Lord, listening to His voice and sharing with each other the impressions you're receiving from Him? Make sure your staff knows, "This is who we are. This is where we are going. We want more of the presence of God."

Also, be certain your congregation understands that your church's prophetic emphasis is not a human invention. This isn't something your leadership team randomly decided to pursue. No, it emerged from prayer and prophetic guidance, and to the best of your ability, God is the architect of all you are building.

3. Make the prophetic a natural part of your church body.

Reinforce who you are as a church again and again. Keep the vision in front of the people and constantly *refocus* them on the church's values, priorities and practices. Do these things in a way that has integrity, cultivates intimacy and brings forth the level of presence and power you long for.

As you walk out these steps, you will be amazed at the prophetic culture that grows in your church body.

2.3

Prophetic Lifestyle

**Focal point: We cultivate an environment where
people encounter God.**

This focal point includes:

- As you build a prophetic culture, your church members become more "naturally supernatural."
- Know your vision; identify and remove challenges to that vision, and share the vision with the body.
- Celebrate and reinforce lifestyles that exemplify your practices.

  Prophecy never came by the will of man, but holy men of God spoke as they were moved by the Holy Spirit.
  — 2 Peter 1:21

What is the true test of your effectiveness in building a prophetic culture? It is whether or not your members are becoming more "naturally supernatural."

As your church adopts a prophetic lifestyle, a set of practices begins to emerge that reflects the things your church does naturally. You don't do them because you are *told* to do them or because you have a program set up that helps you do them. Instead, you do them because you love Jesus, His Word and His purposes, and these things are deeply entrenched in your heart as a community. The values you embraced have become a way of life for you.

How do you promote a prophetic lifestyle in your community?

1. Know your vision.

The first step in building a prophetic lifestyle is knowing your vision for the prophetic and running with it. What is your vision for the prophetic? What do you want to see happen in your church? Begin by incorporating the vision in your own life, and then move on to incorporating it in your leadership team.

Prophets are tuned in to God's presence, strength and imminent purposes. They are especially gifted to hear His voice and to sense what the Holy Spirit is doing at any given time. Prophets are sensitive to God's presence and are champions of His purpose. They take the word of the Lord and run with it in ways that reflect God's presence in the body.

**Prophets reveal God's heart and mind
for the benefit of the Body of
Christ and the fruitfulness of the Church.**

Not only can prophets discern the ways of the Lord, but they also are able to impart that ability to others, either through the laying on of hands or through their anointed teaching. Think about what that means to you on a daily basis. What do you want it to mean for your church?

2. Identify and remove challenges.

Begin to identify challenges that hinder you and your church from living a prophetic lifestyle. In part, that means examining your personal values and priorities and those of your church. What do you truly value? How do you prioritize those values? Are your values and priorities consistent with who Jesus is?

Look at how you manage your money, spend your time and allocate your talents. Are you giving your best for God's purposes? Are you doing so in a balanced way that can be sustained over the long haul?

Does anything need to be adjusted in your life? In your church? Begin to make those adjustments.

3. Share the vision with the body.

Preach on the subject of building a prophetic lifestyle. Talk about it from the pulpit, and encourage a prophetic reality in every context, whether it is in people's homes, small groups, children's church, Sunday morning services, workplaces, government spheres or even the gym.

**In every context, people can cultivate the prophetic,
listen to God for others and communicate what He says.**

Encourage every member of the body to seek revelation, dreams, visions and other kinds of prophetic input from the Spirit of God.

Remember, people emulate what you celebrate. Therefore, celebrate prophecy. Celebrate prophetic leaders in the Body of Christ as well as "regular" members of the church who are moving in the prophetic with words of knowledge, words of wisdom, discerning of spirits and prophetic utterance.

2.4
Prophetic Structures

**Focal point: We build ministries that facilitate
the work of the Holy Spirit.**

This focal point includes:

- Build a bullpen of worship leaders and musicians.
- Understand the importance of intercession, and raise up your intercessors.
- Build prophetic teams and a prophetic community.

> *And so we have the prophetic word confirmed, which you do well to heed as a light that shines in a dark place, until the day dawns and the morning star rises in your hearts.*
> *— 2 Peter 1:19*

Structure can sound like a swear word to many people, especially those who love the presence and power of God. We tend to pit the idea of *structure* against the idea of *spontaneity* when, in actuality, there is no battle between the two. It's like drinking a cup of coffee—we have to have a structure (the cup) in which to hold the coffee and convey it to our mouths. Without that structure, we wouldn't be able to enjoy the coffee. Jesus used the term *wineskin* to describe such a structure and said we needed new wineskins for new wine. As a pastor, if you are trying to bring a greater expression of God's presence and power to your church, you need to build "wineskins" that will support it.

Begin to think strategically, asking, "What kind of groups do we need? What kind of ministries do we need?" At its core, prophetic growth on a church-wide scale looks like new prophetic ministries that allow you to bring the presence of God more effectively and tangibly to your congregation.

At the same time, however, try not to build specialized prophetic groups until you have integrated the prophetic into the general ministries of your church. The two primary venues for general prophetic ministry are your large weekly public meeting and your weekly small group gatherings. Be sure to provide ongoing training in supernatural prophetic ministry in both settings.

Suggested Prophetic Ministries

1. Build a bullpen of worship leaders and musicians.

One key prophetic expression is worship. Worship leaders help us engage God's power and presence; therefore, much of our energy should go into cultivating not just a worship team but a worship *community*. Build a "bullpen" of worship leaders and musicians, and then on a semi-regular basis (every quarter, for instance), meet with those people, hear the voice of God together and set your prophetic goals for that season.

2. Understand the importance of intercession, and raise up your intercessors.

A second important prophetic ministry is intercession. Some church cultures don't put much value in prayer meetings, but until every soul is saved, we have reason to pray and contend. Until every body is healed, we have reason to pray and contend. Obviously, we are not contending *against* God; we are contending *with* Him against circumstantial and demonic forces that are hindering the full expression of His Kingdom. That requires an intercessory process, for the "effective, fervent prayer of a righteous man avails much" (James 5:16).

> **We have a role to play in the intercessory world: We get to partner with God for outcomes.**

Prayer does two things: It truly does shift the heart of God, but it is also the crucible in which our desires are refined. As we seek the Lord, we become more like Him and, therefore, more in tune with Him and what He is doing. Worship and intercession are two ministries Pastor's Coach encourages every church to replicate.

3. Build prophetic teams and a prophetic community.

We also encourage churches to build prophetic teams and prophetic community, both of which can assist people who want to grow in their prophetic gifts. Prophecy can spill over into other ministries at your church as well, such as inner healing; deliverance; and counseling to help individuals overcome past hurts, addictions and other kinds of life-controlling problems. Each of these ministries depends strongly on the prophetic gift.

The key to maintaining prophetic growth
is reinforcing the vision for it again and again.

Tell your church, "These are our values. We are creating culture and a lifestyle that correspond with our values, and we're making prophetic growth a primary purpose of our gatherings so we can experience more of God's presence, power and divine purpose. This will help us become the thriving church He created us to be."

2.5
Prophetic Leadership

**Focal point: We effectively train, release and mentor
new prophetic leaders.**

Steps to building prophetic leadership:

- Identify
- Recruit (according to destiny)
- Train (on the job with supplementary classroom teaching)
- Deploy (transition them into their new roles with care)
- Support (monitor and nurture)

*Blessed is he who reads and those who hear the words of this prophecy,
and keep those things which are written in it; for the time is near.*
— *Revelation 1:3*

New prophetic leaders come out of incubators such as small groups, worship teams, prophetic communities and intercessory teams. It is important to raise them up and work with them to release new expressions of prophetic ministry in your world.

Begin to take note of the individuals in your church who seem to be prophetic: people who are hearing God's voice, receiving words of knowledge and wisdom, having dreams and visions, etc. Once a quarter or even bimonthly, have an "altar call" for prophetically gifted people, and gather them together from time to time and pour into them. Make sure they are part of your overall leadership structure, that they value the whole Body of Christ and that they are part of small groups. In addition to any other ministry they may be doing, they need to be given permission to function prophetically in their small groups and ministry teams. Request and try to maintain permission to speak into their lives, providing guidance and correction when needed.

As you do these things, you will harvest a "crop" of new prophetic gifting that will further prophetic growth in your church.

Leadership Development and Delegation

One of the primary needs in most churches is leadership development and delegation. Although delegation seems like it would be an obvious activity, it can be challenging to implement and carry out effectively. One of the biggest misunderstandings is the difference between leaders and workers. Most pastors will give responsibilities to people—but only as workers. A worker is someone who serves in the presence of his leader, but a *leader* is one who serves in the absence of his leader. In other words, if our delegation is limited to workers who do not directly pastor or develop others, we are not truly delegating; we are just assigning jobs to people.

> **A pastor needs to build a culture of trust and honor**
> **that can support the delegation of leaders who have**
> **true responsibility.**

Keep in mind that true delegation is not merely saying, "Yes," to leaders who lead in your absence—it is also the ability to say, "No," to those who continue to demand your attention, even though they are under one of your delegated leaders. Until you are able to say, "No," and require that members seek care and counsel from their ministry or home group leader, those leaders will be disempowered and you could find yourself sabotaging your growth.

The average church in America is around 60 people. A pastor can care for only so many when she is doing all the work. In order to break this barrier, the pastor needs to lead through leaders, which requires a serious choice: You can *pastor people* or you can *lead leaders*. Ultimately, this is the difference between delegation and development. It's fairly easy to give a task to someone—it is much more intensive to build a developmental relationship with that person. Yet that is what Jesus meant when He commissioned us to make disciples. As leaders, we must become people developers.

For specific steps in how to produce leaders in your church or ministry, please refer to "Raising Up Leaders" in Section 1.5: Apostolic Leadership.

Theme 3
Evangelistic Purpose

**We value the gospel of the Kingdom revealed in the
words and works of Jesus.**

This theme includes:

- God's heart for evangelism (Matthew 9:36)
- Our members are motivated to share their faith with the lost.
- We lead people into full, life-long commitments to Jesus.
- Members are skilled in prophetic and power evangelism.
- We are adding new members through conversion growth.
- We are effectively training, releasing and mentoring new evangelists.

An Introduction to Evangelism

*"For the Son of Man has come to seek and to save that which was
lost."*
— Luke 19:10

A few years ago, we came across a shocking statistic. A study
reported that not a single U.S. county was experiencing conversion-
based church growth that exceeded the region's population growth.
In other words, we may be gaining new members as people move
into our region or transfer directly from other churches—but
generally speaking, we are not doing a good job of winning the lost.
Why is that?

**As leaders, how can we make evangelism
a more prominent expression in our congregations?**

Out of all the priorities of Heaven, nothing compares to the importance of
reaching the lost. Healing can happen in Heaven. Our Christlikeness and
discipleship can be completed in Heaven. But one of the few things we *cannot*

do after we get to Heaven is reach the lost. The salvation of souls is not the only priority in the Kingdom, but in this season it is imminent and urgent.

True Revival and People's Souls

You can find a variety of thoughts on the topic of evangelism. One teaching says that we don't want unbelievers to be reduced to "marks" or conquests. Yes, that's true, but the bottom line is that they *are* our targets. We care about souls, and their eternal destiny hangs in the balance. When Jesus looked upon the multitude, He was moved with compassion. He saw that they were weary and scattered, like sheep without a shepherd (Matthew 9:36). Most of us don't see souls the way Jesus sees souls. We don't tune in at the same level, and we've become somewhat calloused.

**We need to allow our hearts to feel
what Jesus feels and be moved with compassion.**

Another teaching on evangelism incorporates the seven mountains of society and *Victorious Eschatology* (Worldcast Publishing: 2007). We are called to occupy the earth and impact every sphere of society until Jesus comes. It is true that as the reign and peace of Jesus continually increase (Isaiah 9:7), we can expect His Church to grow and become brighter, even if the world gets darker. However, God's power to change the world does not relieve us from the urgency of the times. Every person who has ever lived will have to stand before Jesus and give an account. If the world exists for another 10,000 years—individual existence is only for a short period of time. The point is this: We must understand Heaven's urgency for the salvation of souls.

Hebrews 9:27 tells us, "It is appointed for men to die once, but after this the judgment." If we do not accept Jesus in this life, there is no evidence that we can accept Him after this life. There is no fallback plan. Therefore, the onus is on us to present Jesus in such a way that His beauty and love are unmistakable to seeking hearts. We want people to move from being unreached to reached and meet Jesus face to face.

Again and again, Jesus defined His ministry by saying, "I came to seek and save that which was lost." In its most important sense, "that which was lost" must refer to *those* who are lost. Jesus sent out His disciples to reach the lost and heal the sick, and He commissioned the Church to be His witness to the uttermost parts of the world. Paul's calling was to turn people "from darkness to light, and from the power of Satan to God, that they may receive forgiveness of sins and an inheritance among those who are sanctified by faith" in God (Acts 26:18). We *need* to preach the gospel. It is an urgent task of the Church, and unfortunately, it often goes neglected.

A revival without souls is merely a renewal;
we cannot have true revival without souls.

Ultimately, the mandate to be fruitful, multiply, fill the earth and subdue it is still on the table. We are no longer dealing with *physical* regeneration but *spiritual* regeneration as God works through the Church.

How do we give evangelism a higher place in our hearts? One of the primary steps is connecting with God on this issue. We have to understand the Father's heart for the lost and His purposes for people on the earth. Whether Jesus is coming back in 10 minutes, 10 years or 1000 years, a soul that dies without Him is a soul that is eternally separated from Him. That should grip us at an intense level and compel us to go out into the world and change it.

In order to share God's vision for souls,
we need to know His heart for them.

What If I'm Not Evangelistic?

Not every leader in a church is called to be an evangelist or will function with evangelism as her primary gift, but that doesn't need to hinder the leader from being evangelistic. Even if we don't consider ourselves to be evangelists, we can expand our ability in this area by studying evangelism, learning *how* to evangelize and being around evangelistic people.

Remember, the five aspects of Christ (the quintessential leadership gifts) were given to equip the Church for the work of the ministry (Ephesians 4). These ministry gifts are about equipping the body, and all of us are able to draw from leaders the resources we need to fulfill our roles more effectively. In other words, even if we are not called to be evangelists, we can still draw from evangelistic leaders a measure of "evangelistic grace" that empowers us to be more evangelistic than we would be otherwise. We can read biographies about evangelistic people, meet with evangelistic leaders, attend conferences where evangelistic leaders are speaking, etc. Every time we are around someone who thinks and acts in an evangelistic fashion, it impacts us and enhances our ability to be evangelistic.

We need to be exposed to every aspect of Christ so we can be enhanced in all His aspects.

How Do We Reach People for Jesus?

Here are a few thoughts on how to reach the unreached:

1. As Paul stated in 1 Corinthians 12-14, we need to help outsiders understand our world. Some of us love to host the Holy Spirit, but we don't really know how to host the unreached—people who don't know anything about the Holy Spirit and how His presence can affect people. We don't have to be "seeker sensitive," but we should be "seeker welcoming." We need to train our people how to invite their unsaved friends and prepare them for a supernatural environment. We can carefully explain what God is doing in our public gatherings and not assume new people will automatically "get it." Every church needs to help visitors and new members take incremental steps to greater experience and encounter with God's presence.

2. We need to avoid "hype" and the appearance of hype as much as possible. We live in a cynical, skeptical culture that values authenticity and hates hypocrisy with a passion. Therefore, we need to be open, humble, self-effacing and genuinely caring. Although we cannot cater to the whim of every visitor, if we make it a point to incarnate Jesus in a manner consistent with the people of our city or region, we will be able to bring them to Christ with the fewest obstacles possible.

3. We need to teach our people how to lead others to Jesus. Many believers are able to talk about their faith and salvation, and they may even give prophetic words or pray for someone for healing, but we need to train them how to take the next step and actually lead someone to the Lord. This can be done in simple ways: Model it publicly in altar calls, teach it in classes, and people could also gain experience through basic role-

playing opportunities, where one person pretends to be the minister and the other the seeker. This is the primary work of the evangelist—to equip the saints for evangelism. Consider using a simple tool like the Four Spiritual Laws as a template for personal evangelism.

4. Finally, we need to identify and raise up new evangelists to lead the way in reaching the unreached and equip the saints to minister. Identify the evangelism-oriented people in your church by preaching on the subject and calling forward those whose hearts are burning to respond. Commission them and meet with them again. You could use a gift discovery tool such as www.DestinyFinder.com to help you in the identification process.

As you gather and mentor your emerging evangelists, look for those with a large scope of leadership who are the most effective in winning souls. Once these individuals are identified, pull them aside to form an evangelistic leadership core team who will help you write training materials for the whole church and impart their gifts to others. You could even assign an emerging evangelist to each of your small groups to help the other members reach out to their worlds.

3.1
Evangelistic Vision

Focal point: Our members are motivated to share their faith with the lost.

This focal point includes:

- Have a vision for souls.
- Your vision for evangelism needs to be practical, practiced and celebrated.
- Model the vision personally.
- Make evangelism a priority for your church.

> *Then Jesus went about all the cities and villages, teaching in their synagogues, preaching the gospel of the kingdom, and healing every sickness and every disease among the people. But when He saw the multitudes, He was moved with compassion for them…*
> — *Matthew 9:35-36*

Many churches we coach are concerned because they see *transfer* growth, but not *conversion* growth. Ultimately, this comes down to a matter of vision. We need to have a vision for souls if we are going to reach the people around us.

General Booth, founder of the Salvation Army, once said, "If I could do one thing to complete the training for my people, it would be to dangle them over the lake of fire for 24 hours so that their passion for souls would never be exhausted." The desire to reach the lost begins in the heart; our hearts need to break over those who don't know Jesus. A soul that dies without God's salvation is a soul that is eternally separated from Him—this should grip us at an intense level and compel us to go out into the world to reveal His love.

How to Build a Vision for Evangelism in Your Church

1. Make the vision practical.

Your vision for evangelism needs to be practical, practiced and celebrated. *Practical* simply means that you teach on it regularly and reinforce its different aspects within your church. Like any other vision, the vision for souls is first birthed in the heart of the lead pastor or couple. Even if they are not called as evangelists, the burden for souls starts in them and then spreads to the leadership team.

It is important not only to teach about evangelism, but as a leader you also need to *model* it. If you want your church to have a prophetic lifestyle, for example, emphasize the prophetic within your leadership team and celebrate how God speaks to your core team; celebrate in such a way that it affects the entire church. The same with pastoral care. If you want your church to have a lifestyle of connection and community, celebrate and promote these things as leaders.

**With anything you want to cultivate within your church,
begin in your leadership team.**

2. Model the vision personally.

Incorporate evangelism deeply into your own life. Does your family practice evangelism on a regular basis? Do you as a leader actively share your faith?

Everything you want to bring to your church has to be real inside of you before you can replicate it in others.

3. Make evangelism a priority for your church.

Spend time preaching about evangelism and study it as a congregation, equipping your church to reach the lost. Help your church members learn how to share their personal testimonies, lead people to Jesus and guide others in a sinner's prayer. Encourage your church to reexamine traditional methods of evangelism that have come to be considered "uncool," like the four spiritual laws, tracts, altar calls, etc. Each of these has value. It is time for us to feel God's heart for this topic and tell people about Jesus any way we can.

To break status quo, consider the following options:

- Gather for outreaches once a month and actively seek to experience the urgency and compassion God the Father feels for souls.
- Pray for boldness for one another. Paul asked people to pray that he would increase in boldness (Ephesians 6:19-20), and the early Church prayed a similar prayer in Acts 4.
- Discuss common hindrances to evangelism, such as complacency and compromise. Why do Christians often struggle with these things? What do these things mean? How can you get rid of them in your church?
- Turn the vision of your church toward the harvest, and instill a vision for evangelism within your congregation by whetting their appetites: "What would it look like if you led five people a year to Christ? How would that touch your heart? Who in your world needs Jesus?" Questions like these can be matches dropped on a dry field.

3.2
Evangelistic Culture

Focal point: We lead people into full, life-long commitments to Jesus.

This focal point includes:

- Culture is based in shared values, priorities and practices that unite us.
- Be the change you want to see; make evangelism an active part of your life.
- Make evangelism a priority in your leadership team and church body.
- Create an environment of hospitality for visitors.

> *"In an acceptable time I have heard you,*
> *And in the day of salvation I have helped you."*
> *Behold, now is the accepted time; behold, now is the day of salvation.*
> — *2 Corinthians 6:2*

Part of your responsibility as a senior leader is to introduce your people to God's heart for the lost. You will see amazing results when you can incorporate evangelism into the culture of your church. In this section, we will look at a few ways you can begin to ignite people's hearts for evangelism and build this kind of culture in your church.

John Wimber was convinced that the healthiest churches were grown from the inside out. You can do this by determining what you as a church really care about. What are your values? What things drive you?

Culture is the shared values, priorities and practices, along with the traditions, symbols and expressions, that unite a community. Your culture reflects who your church is at a deep level. As you clarify your values, you establish your priorities—things that are more or less important for how you spend your time, energy and resources. Out of your priorities emerge your everyday practices (things you naturally do on a day-to-day basis). Each of these individual "steps" works to establish a culture of evangelism in your church.

Here are a few other things to consider as you build your church culture:

1. Be the change you want to see.

As a leader, you need to be the first person to change. If you want to build a culture of evangelism in your church, take steps to make evangelism an active part of your routine. Give yourself an easy goal, such as, "I will share my faith with one person a week." That will change your life as a pastor!

Consider making weekly evangelism a requirement for the people on your team, both your elders and your staff. You could approach it like this: "Let's make a commitment. If this is really what we care about, let's see if we can do it."

2. Make evangelism a priority in your church.

A soul that dies without Jesus is a soul that is eternally separated from Him. As that understanding begins to grip your church at an intense level, your members will be compelled to go out and speak to people about Jesus' love.

Once you have perceived God's love for people, translate that understanding into actual lifestyle priorities. Do you have groups that study and practice evangelism? Do you give altar calls at your church? You don't have to do one every week, but do it regularly enough that people know they can bring their unsaved friends to church, and they will have an opportunity to hear the gospel and receive Jesus.

3. Create an environment of hospitality for visitors.

Not everything that happens in a prophetic environment will make sense to visitors. Are your services geared to include non-believers? Begin to bridge the divide in very practical ways. For example, you could include a simple statement in your bulletin: "We value certain things in our church, and we invite you to do whatever is comfortable for you." However you choose to do it, try to create an environment of hospitality for non-Christians and new Christians alike.

Evangelism is such a privilege. We get to show the world that God loves them beyond anything they thought possible.

3.3
Evangelistic Lifestyle

Focal point: We naturally practice proclamation and power evangelism.

This focal point includes:

- Have a vision for souls and motivate people with joy.
- Give people creative ways to reach the lost.
- Provide training so prophetic evangelism becomes a natural part of the body.
- Celebrate all expressions of evangelism in your church.

> *Then He said to His disciples, "The harvest truly is plentiful, but the laborers are few. Therefore pray the Lord of the harvest to send out laborers into His harvest."*
> *— Matthew 9:37-38*

To lead people to Jesus, you need a vision for souls. This vision will come as you seek God's heart for the broken and hurting around you. Let Him share with you the compassion He feels for them, and make sure your congregation knows how much He loves the world.

Here are a few things to consider as you give evangelism a more prominent expression in your congregation:

1. Motivate people with joy.

Joy is a great motivator with a phenomenal amount of power. You can motivate people for a season with duty—or you can motivate them for a lifetime with joy.

Teach on evangelism from the pulpit. Tell your church about the responsibility we have as children of God to share our faith, but don't speak from a place of duty. Instead, help people understand the *joy* they can experience when they go out into the harvest. Jesus declared in Luke 15:7, "I say to you that likewise there will be more joy in heaven over one sinner who repents than over ninety-nine just persons who need no repentance."

**God primarily motivates us through positive means
such as love and delight, rather than rules and duty.**

It's your responsibility to help people discover the delight aspect and strategically wean them from the duty. Activate every member with joy.

2. Be creative in how you share Jesus' love.

Give people creative ways to reach the lost. Help your congregation learn how to share their testimonies and lead people to Jesus. Provide training so prophetic evangelism becomes a natural part of the body. Encourage your church to reexamine even traditional methods of evangelism such as tracts and the four spiritual laws, because we need to tell people about Him in any way we can. It is time for us to know and respond to God's heart for the lost.

One of the easiest ways to tell someone about Jesus is to write out your salvation story and just share it with a friend. "This is how I came to Christ." That is the original gospel tract!

3. Celebrate all expressions of evangelism in your church.

Celebrate the people who are out telling others about Jesus, praying for people and walking in prophetic evangelism. Even if they haven't led anyone to the Lord yet, bring them up to the front of the church and let them talk about their experiences. Every time we celebrate risk, it is valuable and can shift the hearts of the entire church body.

As you reinforce the importance of evangelism, it will become a part of the culture and lifestyle of every individual in your church, and your church will have an extreme impact on your city and region.

3.4
Evangelistic Structures

Focal point: We are adding new members through conversion growth.

This focal point includes:

- You can purposefully structure and spread a heart for souls in your church family.
- Assign an outreach leader to every small group.
- Prepare people to share the gospel at church.
- Set up creative outreaches and make friends with non-believers.

For the wages of sin is death, but the gift of God is eternal life in Christ Jesus our Lord.
— *Romans 6:23*

Do you like the word *structure*?

Many of us in prophetic environments shy away from that word, but the right kinds of structures can propel your church into its destiny. Home groups, ministry groups, children's ministry and so forth can cause an explosion of growth in your church and city.

As your church moves into a culture and lifestyle of evangelism, how can you structure your growth and cause it to increase? Let's look at a few ways you can purposefully create structures that will help spread a heart for souls through your church family.

1. Assign an outreach leader to every small group.

An outreach leader helps his small group stay "outwardly focused." This leader can take simple steps to remind people about the lost. Maybe once a week, that person could share a Scripture about God's heart for the world. He could lead people in prayers for unsaved friends or help other members of the group come up with ways to share their faith. Perhaps every six weeks or so, the small group could do an outreach. No matter the reason or focus of the small group, challenges like this have value and power because they get us out of our comfort zones.

2. Prepare people to share the gospel...at church.

Your church will be visited, or even possibly attended, by people who don't know Jesus very well or at all, so it is good to make sure your main meeting is evangelistic in some way. Your ushers and prayer ministers need to know how to share their faith, should the opportunity arise and people begin asking them questions. Show them a simple process of how to lead someone to Christ.

Your church could also employ more direct routes of spreading the gospel. For example, you could have an evangelism team who goes on regular outreaches to tell people about Jesus. Or you could send the evangelism team out to gather people and bring them to a special meeting, where the church prays for the sick, shares the gospel and leads people to Christ.

3. Set up creative outreaches.

With your leadership team, sit down and come up with different ways your church could have an impact on your city and region. When you think of fun ways of doing outreach, what comes to mind? Be as creative as possible!

You could have individuals in your church whose primary job is to link with other ministries. They could spend time with different missions, after-school programs or on outreaches to the homeless.

You could have specialized groups of people who go into an area, get an apartment together, and live there to have a long-term influence. They could build up the local ministries that already exist there, influence the different spheres (business, government, culture, etc.) in that area, and minister to neighbors. These are just a few ideas.

4. Be strategic and make friends.

Evangelism goes beyond the traditional idea of "outreach" as well. Spread the love of God as you do things in your community. Join community organizations, school boards and other kinds of groups, and build friendships among the unreached, injecting the gospel when the time is right.

Constantly be on the lookout for ways you and your church can create interfaces with the world around you. These days, your "neighborhood" is your workplace, gym, or the neighborhood organization you've joined. We encourage you as a pastor to foster that kind of participation in your community because this will do several things at once:

- It will enliven your church members because they are serving others.
- It will connect the people in your church with non-Christians in a non-religious environment.
- It will act as a bridge for non-Christians to find their way into a church.

3.5
Evangelistic Leadership

Focal point: We are effectively training, releasing and mentoring evangelists.

Steps to building evangelistic leadership:

- Identify
- Recruit (according to destiny)
- Train (on the job with supplementary classroom teaching)
- Deploy (transition them into their new roles with care)
- Support (monitor and nurture)

Therefore, having been justified by faith, we have peace with God through our Lord Jesus Christ.
— *Romans 5:1*

We can't spend much time in the New Testament without realizing an urgency for the gospel. John 3:16 isn't a Christian colloquialism or just a verse all of us memorized in Sunday School—it is our lifeblood, our very foundation.

We carry an incredible message in earthen vessels. Yes, people might reject our message, but that is a very small thing when compared to the benefits that will flood people's lives as they find what their hearts have been seeking: relationship with God.

You can discover the "hidden" evangelists in your congregation by preaching on the topic and calling to the front those whose hearts are stirred. See who responds, pray with these people and then begin to meet with them regularly. Offer them training tools and additional teaching on evangelism and find out what aspects or styles of evangelism make them come alive. Experiment with evangelistic teams, outreaches and events and find out what works for your region and what needs improvement.

For specific steps in how to produce leaders in your church or ministry, please refer to "Raising Up Leaders" in Section 1.5: Apostolic Leadership.

Theme 4
Pastoral Purpose

We value a loving community of care, counsel and Kingdom culture.

This theme includes:

- God's heart for the pastoral gift (Psalm 23; Ezekiel 34; John 21)
- We are a loving community that welcomes and enfolds newcomers.
- We foster care and community in every stage and need of life.
- We provide excellent support for singles, marriages, families and children.
- We host small groups where people minister to one another.
- We effectively train, release and mentor new pastoral leaders.

An Introduction to the Pastoral Gift

The Lord is my shepherd;
I shall not want.
— Psalm 23:1

At the heart of every pastor is the desire to cultivate excellent community— community that responds with counsel, love and true support for its people. Like an experienced shepherd, the pastor helps feed the people, shelters them as they grow, provides for them and protects them spiritually from harm.

Many places in Scripture talk about what it means to be a pastor. One of the most beautiful and thorough descriptions is found in Psalm 23, where David illustrates how a true shepherd functions and how God is the ultimate example of a pastor: He is the good Shepherd who cares for the flock. We see several aspects of the pastoral function in this psalm, and it reveals the heart of God in amazing ways:

- We shall not be in want, which implies there will always be provision.
- God prepares a place for us beside still waters and green pastures.
- He gives us provision, covering and protection.

- He restores our souls.
- He leads us in paths of righteousness.
- He comforts us in death and difficult circumstances.
- He protects us.
- He corrects us.
- He prepares a table before us in the presence of our enemies.
- Goodness and mercy follow us all the days of our lives.
- We will dwell in His house forever.

John 21 is a well-known passage about shepherding, where Jesus talks to Peter about feeding and caring for His sheep. Another pastoral passage is Ezekiel 34, where the shepherds sinned against the Lord by *not* taking care of His flock; they didn't bind up anyone's wounds.

In summary, the pastoral gift has tremendous power and should never be neglected, despite the current emphasis on the apostolic and creating apostolic resource centers. Even though we are in a massive transition from pastoral to apostolic, we don't ever want to minimize the importance of the pastoral role. It is absolutely essential for every healthy church to have thriving community and relationship between its members. The gift of shepherd in the Body of Christ is essential to the wellbeing of God's people and should never be seen as secondary or somehow less important.

Under apostolic leadership pastors create loving community; a sense of connectivity and mutual interdependency; and a place rich in care, counsel and concern.

All members of the Body of Christ need to belong,
and it is the pastoral gift that creates
that sense of belonging and family.

Remember, the pastoral impulse is to gather, care and keep its members, while the apostolic impulse is to gather, train and send people into their God-given destinies. Many believe the existence of the "spectator church" is largely due to an overemphasis of the pastoral gift and an underrepresentation of the apostolic. The Protestant Reformation in the 1500s rediscovered the essential truth of the priesthood of every believer, but unfortunately, Martin Luther's teachings did not restructure the Church as a whole to match the revelation. The message changed…but the "methods of church" continued to be the same. To this day, we have one or two leaders on a stage ministering to a congregation of mostly silent spectators.

Yet God always intended for every member of the body to be a "royal priest" with great gifts and a significant calling, a person who represents Jesus in the congregation and the world beyond. That is the vision that drives the new apostolic reformation!

A Closer Look at Pastoral Care and Small Groups

Even if we don't consider ourselves pastoral, we can expand our pastoral abilities by studying this gift, learning *how* to pastor others and being around pastoral people. Not every church leader is called as a pastor, but pastoring is an essential part of Jesus' ministry in the New Testament and God describes Himself as a Shepherd multiple times in the Old Testament as well. King David learned to shepherd Israel by shepherding his father's flocks, and he described the pastor as a provider, protector, healer, feeder and comforter. According to Ephesians 4:11, pastors exist not only to care for the flock, but they also equip the saints to pastor and care for one another.

Unfortunately, many pastors end up burning out because they try to care for everyone's needs by themselves. The average church in America has only about 60 members (this is often called the "80 barrier") because that is all one person can pastor.

How do we grow beyond this number?

The key to breaking the classic "80 barrier"
is delegating pastoral leadership to others.

Historically, delegated pastoring was done through assistant pastors and adult Sunday School leaders. In the last 40 years, however, it was accomplished primarily through small groups or cell group ministry. Small groups are essential for many reasons. They provide a place for friendship, fellowship and Kingdom community, as well as a context in which growing disciples can minister to one another. Without small groups, many people end up feeling alienated and isolated, but in small groups, most pastoral needs are met without the direct involvement of the pastoral staff. The individual members of the church provide the love, care, healing and blessing that used to be the domain of a single leader.

We recommend building a small group ministry by training leaders and doing a focused small group launch. You can find many great resources to help you with this, and in particular we recommend books by Ralph Neighbour, who offers some good principles on the subject.

4.1

Pastoral Vision

**Focal point: We are a loving community that
welcomes and enfolds newcomers.**

This focal point includes:

- Connect with God, and understand His heart for your church and each individual within your church.
- Ask God for an impartation of His love for people.
- Make a habit of going to the Word of God.
- Write down your vision for community and make it available for your people.
- Celebrate as people walk out the vision.

"The thief does not come except to steal, and to kill, and to destroy. I have come that they may have life, and that they may have it more abundantly. I am the good shepherd. The good shepherd gives His life for the sheep."
— John 10:10-11

What does it mean to have the gift of hospitality? What does it mean to be a welcoming community? How can your church become a family that experiences and expresses true love in a way that makes first-time people feel welcome, yet provides a place of community and belonging for those who have been members for several years?

As the senior leader, you are the custodian of your church's vision. You are the one who is responsible, as a steward, to be sure the vision of a loving community is continually expressed and modeled by the leaders around you. You need to create an atmosphere in which people hear and see the power of transforming community.

Let's look at the ways you can strengthen your church's vision for community.

1. Connect with God.

The first step in building and communicating your vision for a pastoral church is connecting with God. Understand His heart for your church and for each individual within your church. Allow His Spirit to release a fresh vision within you of what it means to be a caring community. Write these things down and go over them on a regular basis.

Pay attention to God's voice (what He tells you in your personal times with Him), as well as the prophetic words you receive. Be open to dreams and visions, and let God's vision for the people you love be implanted in you on a supernatural level.

Loving well is easy in the first stages of pastoral care, but it can get a little harder three, five, seven years down the road. Keep turning to God and asking Him for an impartation of His love for people.

2. Turn to God's Word.

Make a habit of going to the Word of God. Allow your heart to be continually refreshed through Scripture, and study its intricacies.

**When your vision and purpose are founded
in the secret place and the Word of the Lord,
nothing can hinder you from getting to the finish line.**

3. Write and publicize your vision.

Write down your vision for community and make it available for your people. You may even want to rewrite it in different ways because every time you record your vision, you empower people to run with it (see Habakkuk 2). Your people need help remembering *why* they are committed and passionate and why they are making sacrifices. Vision provides a sense of purpose for the pain people go through and the sacrifices they're making. Keep declaring, "This is who we are. This is where we're going. This is the kind of love we want to express." This will help people commit themselves to the vision and exemplify it.

Also, use outside sources to confirm your vision, which can be done in a number of ways. Keep your ear to the ground and study the Body of Christ as a whole. Understand your mentors; are you in alignment with the leaders above you in your movement? Are you in some degree of connection with the other pastors in your city? Is your vision reflected across the Body of Christ? Obviously, God gives different visions to different churches, but you will often be able to see how your vision fits in the bigger picture of what God is doing in the rest of your city and region.

4. Celebrate as people walk out the vision.

As your vision becomes known, celebrate those who are walking it out. Even from the pulpit, you can take a moment to point people out: "Sister So-and-So took a meal over to the Joneses when they were sick." Or, "Brother So-and-So is trying to make sure the people under him at his job have a real sense of connection and community." In a thousand different ways, you can illustrate how to do community well with close-to-home, real-life examples. Remember that people will emulate what you celebrate, so make sure you have on-going testimonies of those who are successfully creating community.

4.2
Pastoral Culture

**Focal point: We foster care and community in
every stage and need of life.**

This focal point includes:

- Clarify your values, priorities and practices.
- Make true and tender care a part of your culture.
- Have a strong value for God's Father-heart.
- Infuse pastoral culture into your primary team and congregation.

> *"I am the good shepherd; and I know My sheep, and am known by My
> own."*
> — John 10:14

God is entirely motivated by love. Love moves His hands to action and is the driving force of His heart. Our freedom is a pulsing desire within Him. Building a pastoral culture in your church will help each member walk in the freedom and love God has made available to us.

Remember, *culture* is the shared values, priorities and practices, along with the traditions, symbols and expressions, that unite a community. Your culture reflects who your church is at a deep level. As you clarify your values, you establish your priorities—things that are more or less important for how you spend your time, energy and resources. Out of your priorities emerge your everyday practices (things you naturally do on a day-to-day basis). Each of these individual "steps" works to establish a pastoral culture in your church.

How to Build a Pastoral Culture in Your Church

Many apostolic churches that are strong in the prophetic tend to neglect care and community, but we should never do one and leave the other undone. The Church represents the Good Shepherd on the earth; therefore, true and tender care needs to be a part of our culture.

1. Have a strong value for God's Father-heart.

To build a culture that cares, we need to consider the passion of God's heart and have a value for fathering, which essentially looks like valuing the innocent and helpless among us. We also need to honor sacrifice and practical love, which is love in action toward one another. These things have a tremendous payoff, and they cannot be left to chance. We have to work at them as a congregation and cause them to grow.

Look closely at the five core values of caring community (providing, protecting, healing, feeding and comforting) and begin to emphasize and implement them, adapting your church language, practices and priorities to support them.

2. Infuse pastoral culture into your primary team.

As a leader, give your core team a vision and infuse them with the values and priorities that will help them take the vision as their own and spread it through the congregation. Remember, culture reflects the senior leader's lifestyle and the core community of the leadership team.

3. Bring pastoral culture to your congregation.

Show your church what it looks like to walk in loving community with one another.

Begin to instill pastoral culture in your congregation through personal interaction, public preaching, testimonies and ongoing celebration of cultural successes. As you do these things, you will see pastoral culture form. Every movement needs pastors; they are connectors who naturally link a group together in community.

4.3
Pastoral Lifestyle

Focal point: We provide excellent support for singles, marriages, families and children.

This focal point includes:

- Raise up the vision for care and community.
- Identify and remove challenges.
- Encourage friendships in your church.

  When the Chief Shepherd appears, you will receive the crown of glory that does not fade away.
  — 1 Peter 5:4

When you look at the body of believers in your care, do you see the pastoral gift at work among them? The following questions might give you a glimpse of the "pastoral state" of your congregation:

- How inclined are the people toward fellowship?
- Do they enjoy just hanging out with one another?
- How much do they want to be together?
- Do they spend time together having fun over a meal, opening up their hearts and homes to one another? Is this a natural value (lifestyle) among your people?

Let's look at a few ways you can build a lifestyle of pastoral care in your church.

1. Raise up the vision for care and community.

Ultimately, church programs don't endure unless a lifestyle is already in place that supports them. To build a pastoral lifestyle among your people, teach about pastoring and show them what it looks like—model it for them. We need to celebrate the actual pastors in our midst, and we also need to celebrate the "regular" members of the church who are moving in pastoral ways (purposefully connecting with one another, caring for one another when people are sick or after surgeries, etc.).

Your senior leader and leadership team need to make a conscious effort to model the pastoral gift in everyday settings. To the extent these values happen in the leadership team is the extent to which they happen in the congregation. As leaders, we have an amazing opportunity to mirror the heart of Jesus as we encourage those around us in family and community.

2. Identify and remove challenges.

The Bible tells us to love the Lord our God with all our hearts, souls, minds and strength, and to love our neighbor as ourselves. The law and the prophets are summed up in that one thought: Love one another (Matthew 22:37-40). The power of the pastoral gift is found in that love-one-another command. Your church members are gripped by the same love and care for the same vision, which means they can walk together in pastoral harmony that leads them into God's purposes.

Begin to identify challenges that might hinder you and your church from living a pastoral lifestyle. That often means examining your own values and priorities. What do *you* truly value? Look at how you manage your money, spend your time and allocate your talents to get a good idea of your priorities.

Does anything need to be adjusted in your life? In your church? Begin to make those adjustments.

3. Encourage friendships in your church.

It may sound trite to encourage your church members to "make friends" with one another, yet the power of the pastoral gift is found in love. For the Body of Christ to function properly, we need connection and family. Pastors care deeply about each individual in the church and help people feel honored, connected and fulfilled in their participation. We cannot force people to be friends with one another, but we can create an environment where friendships happen naturally. We can cultivate relationships that go beyond cultural and even personal barriers, so we can find true joy with our spiritual family.

4.4
Pastoral Structures

Focal point: We host small groups where people minister to one another.

This focal point includes:

- Pastoral ministry is woven into every aspect of the church.
- The church is a "hospital" for ill or injured people who need care, "physical therapy" and restoration.
- Every church needs ministries that support the family.
- The best way to build caring community is through your home group ministry.

  May the God of peace who brought up our Lord Jesus from the dead, that great Shepherd of the sheep, through the blood of the everlasting covenant, make you complete in every good work to do His will.
  — Hebrews 13:20-21

Jesus is the Good Shepherd. He is the One who supports us, leads us, guides us, feeds us and restores our souls when we are weary and broken, and every church should reflect His heart of care and love.

All of us are involved in caring for one another. Pastoral ministry is woven into every aspect of the church, whether you're a senior leader, parking attendant, janitor, worship leader or children's ministry worker.

Other portions of Pastor's Coach will provide in-depth ministry training in different aspects of church life and programs, but in this assessment, let's talk about three ministry categories we believe every church should implement in order to grow in pastoral care.

Hospital Ministries

A church is a hospital of sorts for ill or injured people who need care, "physical therapy" and restoration. This hospital includes your prayer ministries and supportive inner healing and counseling ministries, which integrate God's power and presence to touch people's lives in significant ways. Every church should host these types of pastoral expressions or be able to direct people where to find them.

Family Ministries

Every church needs ministries that support the family. Here are a few common examples of community-building ministries that can help nurture the church family:

- Children's ministry
- Nursery ministry
- Youth ministry
- Premarital counseling
- Small group connectivity

Home Groups

The best way to build loving community is through your home group ministry. A home group is not just a place of community, care, counsel and discipleship, but it is the place where each person's gifts can be drawn out. Home groups function best when they are apostolic in nature and therefore are focused on the multiplication of new leaders, new ministries and helping people discover their gifts.

At Pastor's Coach, we recommend that every church have a growing small group (also called cell group) ministry. Try to have at least 70 percent of Sunday's attendance be involved in small groups. Obviously, this takes work and time to accomplish, but as you put this ministry in place and watch it grow, you will never regret the rewards you receive as a church.

4.5
Pastoral Leadership

Focal point: We effectively train, release and mentor new pastoral leaders.

Steps to building pastoral leadership:

- Identify
- Recruit (according to destiny)
- Train (on the job with supplementary classroom teaching)
- Deploy (transition them into their new roles with care)
- Support (monitor and nurture)

For you were like sheep going astray, but have now returned to the Shepherd and Overseer of your souls.
— *1 Peter 2:25*

Who are you raising up? Who is your legacy?

Look at your congregation and try to identify the individuals who have pastoral callings. You could use a gift assessment tool like the one we offer at www.DestinyFinder.com to help you identify the gifts and callings of individuals in your church. As you preach on pastoral care and the shepherd's heart, from time to time do "altar calls" for those who believe they are called to pastoral ministry and see who responds.

Gather these individuals together periodically and pour into them. Make sure they are part of your overall leadership structure, that they value the whole Body of Christ and that they are part of small groups. Put them in positions of leadership that will highlight their gifting so they can be more impactful. In addition to any other ministry they may be doing, they need to be given permission to function pastorally in their small groups.

Help people discover themselves as caregivers. There are people in your congregation who may be more "people oriented" than you, and they can be trained as connectors who create a sense of love and community in your church. Foster that kind of relationship with your team.

For specific steps in how to produce leaders in your church or ministry, please refer to "Raising Up Leaders" in Section 1.5: Apostolic Leadership.

Theme 5
Teaching Purpose

We value the power of truth that brings teaching, training and transformation.

This theme includes:

- God's heart for the teaching gift (Psalm 1; Ephesians 4; Hebrews 4:12)
- Our members are biblically literate and theologically informed.
- Our members value Scripture study on an individual and corporate level.
- We provide intensive, personal discipleship for new and growing believers.
- Every member is equipped to equip others with the truth of Scripture.
- We effectively train, release and mentor new gifted teachers.

An Introduction to the Teacher Gift

Oh, how I love Your law!
It is my meditation all the day.
— Psalm 119:97

Through the books of Moses, the Psalms, Jesus' life on earth and the epistles, it is clear that loving the Word of the Lord is a key to knowing and walking with Him.

- Psalm 1 talks about those whose delight is in the law of the Lord and who meditate on that law night and day.
- In the beginning was the Word, and the Word was with God and the Word was God. Jesus said, "My words are spirit and they are life" (John 6:63).

- The Word of God is alive and powerful, sharper than any two-edged sword (Hebrews 4:12). We need to understand the importance of the Word and learn to love it with all our hearts.

In standard charismatic teaching, two distinct words describe the way God speaks. *Logos* usually refers to the eternal, firm Word of God, which is our plumb line and point of reference. *Rhema* normally refers to the momentary word of the Lord—that is, it is the word God speaks prophetically through the "still, small voice" within people or through the use of spiritual gifts. The prophetic word of the Lord must never contradict the written Word of the Lord. The gift and ministry of the teacher are absolutely essential to upholding Scripture (*logos*) as we continue to grow in the gift and ministry of prophecy (*rhema*).

Teachers are entrusted with the Word of God at a special level. Jesus Himself was called the Great Teacher. After the Church was formed, His followers continued in the apostles' teaching, fellowship, the breaking of bread and prayer (Acts 2:42). They delved into the Word of God. Paul, who was truly a teacher's teacher, laid out the aspects of redemption with a beautiful and precise perfection. Look at the way he handled questions of salvation in the book of Romans, or the nature of the Church and of the believer's identity in Ephesians. His teachings are profoundly insightful and a model for every teacher.

Teaching is not merely the articulation of ideas and principles, but it is a supernatural activity by which an anointed teacher can bring words of affirmation to the human heart. A person gifted in teaching has the God-given ability to take truth, break it into bite-sized pieces and deliver it to the very point of the human heart where confusion and deception have occurred. The teacher can release the truth that displaces the lie and bring the hearer into the freedom Jesus described when He said, "The truth shall make you free."

Just as the evangelist is centered on the good news and salvation of the lost, and the pastor is centered on love and community, the teacher is centered on truth and the power of truth to bring transformation.

**Keys to the teacher's heart are communicating
and conveying truth for training and transformation.**

Unfortunately, in prophetic movements the teacher gift can end up being disregarded. It was the predominant gift in the Body of Christ for years, and those who could declare sound doctrine were considered the pinnacle of leadership. This led the Body of Christ to focus more on the letter of the law, not life in the Spirit. Thankfully, the majority of us have come out of that, but we need to be careful we do not correct too far. As Jesus said, truth sets us free. It isn't the truth we *hear* that makes us free; it is the truth that confronts falsehood inside us—truth that deals with the lies and evicts them from our hearts. That is the truth that actually has value. This requires an anointed teacher, who can bring truth to the human heart.

What If I'm Not a Teacher?

Even if we don't consider ourselves to be teachers, we can expand our ability to teach by studying the teaching gift, learning how to be teachers and being around people who are gifted in this area.

The quintessential leadership gifts of Ephesians 4 focus on equipping the Body of Christ. All of us are able to draw from anointed teachers the resources we need to fulfill our roles more effectively. Even if we are not called to be teachers ourselves, we can still extract from them a measure of "grace" in this area that empowers us to be better teachers than we would be naturally.

Remember, we need to be exposed to every aspect of Christ so we can be enhanced in all His aspects.

5.1
Vision for Truth

**Focal point: Our members are biblically literate
and theologically informed.**

This focal point includes:

- Have a vision that will cause people to understand the power of the Word and bring them into right alignment with it.
- Your vision for the Word of God needs to be practical, practiced and celebrated.
- Vision for the Word is first birthed in the heart of the lead pastor or couple.
- Make your vision for the Word a priority for your staff and church.

> *But his delight is in the law of the Lord,*
> *And in His law he meditates day and night.*
> — *Psalm 1:2*

The Bible is our hub, mandate and launching point; it is our final constitution in the Kingdom of Heaven. The Scriptures are our full and final authority on true faith and practice. All of us need to wrap our hearts around the Word of God and be transformed by His awesome truth.

As a leader, have a vision that will cause people to understand the power of the Word and bring them into right alignment with it. Your vision for the Word needs to be put on display again and again.

How to Build a Vision for God's Word in Your Church

1. Make your vision for the Word practical.

Your vision for the Word of God needs to be practical, practiced and celebrated. A special gift, teachers see God's purposes in His Word and are able to communicate them in such a way that they are added to the Body of

Christ's knowledge base and practice. Not only are they anointed to teach the Word, but these gifted men and women are also anointed to impart love of the Word, and even the ability to teach, to other people.

As a leader, you get to echo the heart of Jesus as you encourage those around you to go deep into His Word.

2. Model your vision.

Like any vision, vision for the Word is first birthed in the heart of the lead pastor or couple. Even if they are not called as teachers, love for the Word of God starts in them and then spreads to the leadership team.

Embed love for the Word in your own life. Does your family study the Word together on a regular basis? Do you as a leader actively seek to connect with God in the pages of His book?

Speak to your core team about spending time in God's Word. Build up vision for the Word within them. Perhaps you and your leadership team could go to conferences and on retreats that are focused on the Word. Actively seek ways you and your team could fall more in love with God's Word.

3. Make your vision for the Word a priority for your staff and church.

Spend time preaching about God's Word and study it as a congregation. Equip your church to really delve into its truth, and reveal how you use the Word to guide your decision-making processes. Counsel others with Scripture and hold people to the Word. Inspire them and show them how powerful the Word of God can be in daily life.

Celebrate the Word in personal areas of independent study, meditation and memorization. Also celebrate the actual teachers in your midst (those in the office of teacher), as well as the "regular" members of the church who love God's Word and are sharing His truths with others.

As you do these things, you reinforce value for the Word, strengthening and upholding your vision for a church that loves Scripture.

5.2

Culture of Truth

**Focal point: Our members value Scripture study
on an individual and corporate level.**

This focal point includes:

- Clarify your values, priorities and practices.
- Personify the culture yourself.
- Infuse love for the Word into your primary team.
- Bring love for the Word to your congregation.

> *For the word of God is living and powerful, and sharper than any two-edged sword, piercing even to the division of soul and spirit, and of joints and marrow, and is a discerner of the thoughts and intents of the heart.*
> — *Hebrews 4:12*

The teacher's powerful love for God's Word can spread through your entire church. As you build a culture around this love for the Word, God's truth will become a firm, established part of your congregation.

Remember, *culture* is the shared values, priorities and practices, along with the traditions, symbols and expressions, that unite a community. Your culture reflects who your church is at a deep level. What does your church value more than anything? What drives you as a congregation? As a body, what things have you proven you care about again and again? As you clarify your values, you establish your priorities—things that are more or less important for how you spend your time, energy and resources. Out of your priorities emerge your everyday practices (things you naturally do on a day-to-day basis). Each of these individual "steps" works to establish in your church a culture that loves God's Word.

Here are a few other things to consider as you build your church culture:

1. As a leader, personify the culture yourself.

Make the love and study of Scripture a priority. Incorporate love for the Word in your own life. Consider the following questions:

- How has the Word impacted you?
- How has it impacted your family and friends?
- Does your family study the Word together on a regular basis?
- Do you as a leader actively seek to connect with God through His Word?

As God's Word becomes more real to you and you share your love for it with those you are leading, it will become more real to them as well.

2. Infuse love for the Word into your primary team.

Live in a culture that honors Scripture. What are the values that undergird your belief that God is true? What are the values that illustrate integrity, consistency and intelligence in the Kingdom of God? How could you reveal your love for the Word on a daily basis? All of these factors have value, and you can promote them to strengthen a culture that upholds God's Word.

Realize the role of intellect and reason in the biblical process. Part of the greatest commandment (Matthew 22:37-38) is loving God with all our *minds*. The enlightened mind is not in opposition to the Holy Spirit, for the Bible says we are transformed by the renewing of our minds (Romans 12:2). We need to realize that when God says, "Come, let us reason together," He is talking about a mental process. It is unwise to depend solely on revelation or a vision—we also need to depend on what the Bible says as revealed through the gifted teacher.

3. Bring love for the Word to your congregation.

Begin to instill in your congregation a culture that loves God's Word and revels in it through personal interaction, public preaching, testimonies and ongoing celebration of cultural successes.

Teachers are anointed to impart love of the Word. This often occurs through public teaching in classrooms and large group settings. However, a teacher's most basic work is to communicate truth to individual members of the Body of Christ. That is the foundation of the teacher gift, and we call it discipleship.

5.3
Lifestyle of Truth

**Focal point: We provide intensive, personal discipleship
for new and growing believers.**

This focal point includes:

- Know your vision for the Word.
- Raise up the vision of love for God's Word.
- Share the vision with the body, and encourage every believer to be in the Word as much as possible.

*Great peace have those who love Your law,
And nothing causes them to stumble.*
— Psalm 119:165

Teachers are knowledgeable people who seek to understand facts. They care deeply about the truth and comprehend the power of truth to set people free and help them thrive. Love for the Word of God courses through their veins. In church settings, you often find gifted teachers teaching Scripture and lifestyle classes and providing detailed training. Along the way, they impart their gift and love for the Word to others.

Let's look at a few ways you can start to build in your church a lifestyle that honors and loves the Word of God.

1. Know your vision for the Word.

What is your vision for the Word of God? Psalm 1:2 says,

*But his delight is in the law of the Lord,
And in His law he meditates day and night.*

Teachers love Scripture—what Psalm 1:2 calls the *law* of the Lord—and were created to minister God's truth in a loving way to others. Lives are changed as a lifestyle of loving the Word is embraced and established in a church. As leaders, we get to reveal God's heart as we encourage those around us to go deep into God's Word and to teach others to do the same.

2. Identify and remove challenges.

God's purpose in the teacher gifting is to bring forth His reality (His truth) in a way that produces transformation. God's word is truth (John 17:17), and Jesus *personifies* truth because He is the ultimate reality. In Jesus, there is an incredible connection to what is absolutely real.

Does anything hinder your church from living a lifestyle that is passionate for God's Word and His truth? You may need to examine your values and priorities. What do you value? How do you prioritize those values? Look at how you manage your money, spend your time and allocate your talents—are you giving your best for the purposes God created? Are you doing so in a balanced way that is sustainable over the long haul? If anything needs to be adjusted in your life or church, begin to make those adjustments.

3. Share your vision for the Word with the body.

To grow in your church a lifestyle that loves God's Word, encourage every believer to be in the Word as much as possible. People need to make Scripture a part of them and explore its pages to truly comprehend and experience it. As they begin to understand its worth, the Word comes alive in their hearts and they learn how to "feast" on Scripture in a way that excites and inspires them to share it with others.

The Bible tells us to "reprove, rebuke, exhort with great patience and instruction" (2 Timothy 4:2, NASB), and we also need to be able to give an answer for the hope that lies within us (1 Peter 3:15). Every believer is called to share what she is learning, which is an aspect of the teacher gift.

5.4

Structures of Truth

**Focal point: Every member is equipped to equip
others with the truth of Scripture.**

This focal point includes:

- Offer adult classes that teach the Word.
- Help people own what they learn.
- Have leaders train up leaders in small-group settings.
- Make sure you're doing it first.

> *If you really fulfill the royal law according to the Scripture, "You shall
> love your neighbor as yourself," you do well.*
> — *James 2:8*

How do you ignite passion in people's hearts for the Word of God? Let's
look at a few hands-on, practical ways you can help grow a deep love for
God's Word in your congregation.

1. Offer adult classes that teach the Word.

Some people in prophetic communities dismiss the idea of structure,
believing it flies in the face of flowing with the Spirit and being spontaneous.
But that isn't necessarily true. Structure is the vehicle that helps us deliver and
produce what we want the church to grow in. For instance, a discipleship
class is a structure that can help people learn more about Jesus and begin to
walk in deeper intimacy with Him. Though the class is a planned group
(something structured), the outcome of taking the class is greater intimacy
and understanding how to flow with the Spirit.

You can build simple, "easy" structures throughout your church that help
communicate and teach Scripture. Though most transformation doesn't take
place in a classroom, the necessary *fuel* for transformation can.

Many churches build schools of ministry to communicate God's Word, a lifestyle of revival and other key elements. With any school you build, however, remember you still need to have real-life contact between parents and children—that is, between disciple-makers and people who are seeking training.

2. Help people own what they learn.

Create within your people a sense of ownership of Scripture. What they are learning needs to take root inside them and be carried out the door with them when they leave each day: "I'm going to this class, and I'm learning these things and I own them; they're a part of me, and I'm committed to carrying them and giving them away to others." That sense of ownership is crucial. It should be a goal of every church to have all members ready and trained to equip others with Scripture.

3. Have leaders train up leaders in small-group settings.

Self-multiplying structures such as home groups disciple people and help them grow in skill, experience and relationship. In whatever ministry, group or class you are leading, train up your replacement (for the purpose of replicating the group and starting new groups). Encourage your trainees; disciple them and let them teach portions of the class as they are able.

Don't neglect the power of small groups as a primary delivery system for every aspect of Christ. Make sure your people are invested in small groups, communicating with each other and processing Scripture together as a normal part of their Christian life/community experience.

4. Make sure you're doing it first.

Living things grow from the inside out. Build structures that begin in the heart and grow out from the center. Make the love and study of Scripture a priority in your own life. Do
this at home and with your staff first, and then try to build it in the lives of the next generation of leaders, so they in turn can do it with other people in your church.

Make sure your structures are organic and flourishing from the inside out, so the members of your church can be fully equipped for every good work in Christ. In this way your church can bring transformation to the world around you.

5.5
Teachers in Leadership

**Focal point: We effectively train, release
and mentor new gifted teachers.**

Steps to building teachers among your leadership:

- Identify
- Recruit (according to destiny)
- Train (on the job with supplementary classroom teaching)
- Deploy (transition them into their new roles with care)
- Support (monitor and nurture)

> *Your word is very pure;*
> *Therefore Your servant loves it.*
> *— Psalm 119:140*

Do you know who the gifted teachers are in your church? What can you do to engage with them and promote love for God's Word among your people?

Unfortunately, teachers don't always survive well in prophetic environments because they love the Word of God so much and can become offended if Scripture seems to be undervalued. We encourage you to look for these people. Celebrate them and pull them up to a new level of participation.

Bible schools and seminaries exist primarily for those who are called to teach—they train teachers. Obviously, not every teacher has to go to seminary, but we recommend that those who are called to teach consider doing so because of the strong foundations these schools can lay in the teacher's gift and spiritual abilities.

For specific steps in how to produce leaders in your church or ministry, please refer to "Raising Up Leaders" in Section 1.5: Apostolic Leadership.

Theme 6
Kingdom Administration

We value administrative excellence in managing ministry and mission.

This theme includes:

- God's heart for wise administration (Acts 6; 2 Peter 1:3; Romans 12:2)
- We promote a vision for excellence in the church.
- Our culture supports development and growth from "glory to glory."
- We live in a way that doesn't overextend our resources.
- We uncover what we need and work together for growth.
- We effectively train, release and mentor new gifted administrators.

An Introduction to the Administrative Gift

His divine power has granted to us everything pertaining to life and godliness, through the true knowledge of Him who called us by His own glory and excellence.
— 2 Peter 1:3 (NASB)

One of the gifts of the Spirit, administration is an important and powerful part of Kingdom reality. It is spoken of in 1 Corinthians 12:28 and Romans 12:7-8, and throughout Scripture administrators had high value. They coordinated, mobilized and moved things forward for the nation of Israel and the Body of Christ as a whole.

Those who manage the army's logistics and tactics are vital, and unfortunately, many churches have experienced various kinds of failures because of poor administration and the unwise allocation of resources. Administrators steer groups toward a goal and allow resources to be channeled in such a way that maximum impact is achieved.

Jesus depended on administrators while He walked the earth. Certain women traveled with Him and helped administrate His group in practical, logistical ways (see Luke 8). Later in the book of Acts, Greek widows were not being served well, and the apostles realized the need for administrators. So in Acts 6 they set aside servants who helped administrate practical matters. The word *deacon* isn't used in Acts 6, but the deaconal role began through this event with the Greek widows.

Many churches don't use the word *deacon* anymore, preferring to call people staff or workers, but in the New Testament, the elder and the deacon were the two primary job descriptions. The elder is called to pastor and oversee *people*, while the deacon oversees projects and functions. *Diakonos*, which we translate as *deacon*, means the ability to serve and administrate on someone else's behalf. It is the person who is good with numbers, details and keeping an organization running smoothly.

The administrator's realm is vast,
because every gift has an administrative dimension.

Pastors, evangelists, prophets, teachers and apostles need to mobilize others and have people do certain tasks. They need help writing budgets; allocating time, energy and money; keeping calendars and schedules; and a host of other details. Some people look at everything that needs to be done and panic—but administrators are gifted in seeing the details and orchestrating them in a way that lets the ship sail forward smoothly.

In essence, the administrator's realm is the ministry of excellence working within the quality of how we manage our resources and accomplish our goals in the most effective, efficient way.

What Lies Beyond

Not only do administrators help a church with its present needs, but they are also able to look into the future. They see the steps that need to be taken so the end goal can be reached, and they plan accordingly.

God has called us to go out and change the world.

This requires us to move beyond just managing what we have *right now* and begin to perceive what lies ahead. We can marshal our resources in a way that allows for future management.

A Note on Administration vs. Kingdom Strategy

Administration and strategic planning are similar gifts, but they are different enough that we included them as separate themes in this assessment. Administration (theme six) is the management of resources, projects, facilities and finances that facilitate the church's ministries and care for its members.

On the other hand, Kingdom strategy (theme seven) is more futuristic. It sees where the church or ministry is *going* versus where it is right now. You could say that administration is management, while strategic planning is projection.

As you go through this theme, keep in mind your finances, facilities, calendar, media and Internet. Are the following statements true of your church?

- We encourage and practice wise and faith-filled financial stewardship.
- Our facilities are functional and well suited to fulfill our mission and vision.
- We manage our calendar effectively in light of our purpose and priorities.
- We effectively share our message through various forms of media.
- Our website is creative, accurate, comprehensive, current and well used.

6.1
Vision for Administrative Excellence

Focal point: We promote a vision for excellence in the church.

This focal point includes:

- The vision for administration is excellence in everything you do.
- Make the vision practical.
- Make your vision for excellence a priority for your staff and church.
- As a church, be excellent stewards.

> *And He is before all things, and in Him all things consist.*
> *— Colossians 1:17*

God is an administrator. He runs a universe of a hundred billion planets and He's good at it. There is order and structure, growth and purpose. Organizational excellence depends on wise administration and strategic planning.

Simply stated, the vision for administration is excellence in everything we do. We are a people of high quality who reflect the excellence of our Father and the Kingdom of Heaven. The quality of our work and lives should be in a continual process of improvement because we are moving from "glory to glory" even in practical matters.

As leaders, we want to promote a vision for excellence in our congregations. We should never do anything halfway. Why not? Because we know the Creator of the universe! We are tied into the heart, mind and Word of God; therefore, we should be so clearly gifted in administration and planning that we are always one step ahead of the world in terms of the implementation of excellence. We can be leaders in the spheres to which God has called us. The world should look to us for the best songs, the best movies, the best political solutions, the best societal and economic solutions. We don't mimic the world—we lead the world.

How to Promote a Vision for Excellence in Your Church

1. Make the vision practical.

Why is it important to promote excellence in everything you do? What is your own personal vision for excellence?

Show the church why you love doing things well, how it has affected your life and how it can change theirs. What are some practical steps you can take to promote a vision for administration and the spirit of excellence in your church? Begin by preaching about a high vision for excellence. Let people hear about the vision in regular church services, and also let them see the vision in action in every possible area within the church. For example, proof your weekly bulletin and overheads for typos and missing words. When you hand out sermon notes or other publications, make sure they are in order. Everything from public relations to the church's website to the way you run Sunday mornings and the greeting ministries—every aspect of ministry should reflect your administrative values for excellence, effectiveness and efficiency of use.

2. Make your vision for excellence a priority for your staff and church.

In order to make excellence a deep, core value in your congregation, it first needs to be a deep, core value to you and your leadership team. Celebrate excellence in your leadership group in such a way that your vision for it extends to the rest of the church. As people see the importance of excellence, they will naturally begin to adopt it as a value in their own lives.

3. As a church, be excellent stewards.

Be a good steward with what you've been given. A crucial issue, money is a point where the world is offended with the Body of Christ, when it could be a point where we are examples of wise stewardship. Most churches tend to consume 80-90 percent of their income just to keep afloat and then provide subpar services for their congregations. The world's non-profit organizations, meanwhile, tend to pour about 90 percent of their resources back into the community to help bring change and improvement. How are you giving back to your community? How are you blessing and being generous with your neighbors, even those who don't attend your church or don't agree with you? It is vital that your church is excellent in matters of generosity.

The more the Body of Christ becomes an apostolic resource center, the more we will find ourselves able to promote Kingdom reality in efficient and effective ways.

6.2

Culture of Administrative Excellence

**Focal point: Our culture supports development
and growth from "glory to glory."**

This focal point includes:

- As a prophetic people, we can be good stewards of our time, energy and talents.
- Culture reflects the senior leader's lifestyle and the core community of the leadership team.
- Begin to instill a culture of excellence in your congregation.
- Focus on building a culture that allows for development and growth from "glory to glory."

> *"His lord said to him, 'Well done, good and faithful servant; you were faithful over a few things, I will make you ruler over many things. Enter into the joy of your lord.'"*
> *— Matthew 25:21*

It isn't necessary for prophetic cultures to constantly "shoot from the hip," so to speak. We can be prophetic *and* good stewards of our time, energy and talents. We can be prophetic *and* produce excellent material, products and resources that benefit the people we are trying to reach.

Remember, *culture* is the shared values, priorities and practices, along with the traditions, symbols and expressions, that unite a community. Your culture reflects who your church is at a deep level. As you clarify your values, you establish your priorities—things that are more or less important for how you spend your time, energy and resources. Out of your priorities emerge your everyday practices (things you naturally do on a day-to-day basis). Each of these individual "steps" works to establish a culture of excellence in your church.

Here are a few other things to consider as you build your church culture:

1. Determine your values and priorities.

Culture reflects the lifestyle of the senior leader and leadership team. Therefore, the first step in cultivating a culture of excellence is for you to look at your own values and priorities. Determine the values that promote excellence, such as the glory of God (that which clearly reveals Him) and generosity (which clearly models stewardship and relational integrity). What you value is the intangible basis that helps you determine what is truly important to you.

Ask yourself these questions:

- Am I thinking about my people developmentally?
- Am I taking the time to work with them?
- Is my desire for excellence in the church integrated into my values, priorities and practices as a leader?

2. Share the vision for change and excellence.

As a leader, give your people a vision for excellence and infuse them with the values and priorities that will help them become promoters of excellence in their own right. You can begin to instill a culture of excellence in your congregation through personal interaction, public preaching, testimonies and the ongoing celebration of excellence wherever it is found.

3. Be excellent in what you do as a church.

Focus on building a culture that allows people to develop and grow from "glory to glory" (2 Corinthians 3:18). One way to do this is through *inspection*. It's a good idea to have at least three sets of eyes read everything you publish, both printed material and anything that will appear online. That may seem like a simplistic idea to you, but if you find 10 typos on someone's website, what will happen to your respect for that organization? It will go down. Mistakes happen, but the more we keep them from happening, the better. "Small" things like typos work against a culture of administrative excellence.

As another example, issues with bookkeeping will also lead people to question a church's administrative excellence. Keep superb records and inspire your people to do the same. Try to consider excellence in practical ways. If your ushers are not in place or if your announcement people aren't in tune with the congregation, these are inconsistencies that will eventually have a significant effect on your presentation. All of these issues are important.

The ministry of excellence also includes practical structures such as serving the poor or running the bookstore or food program. Encourage these structures, and whenever possible model excellence for your congregation.

6.3
Lifestyle of Administrative Excellence

Focal point: We live in a way that doesn't overextend our resources.

This focal point includes:

- Just as God is excellent in everything He does, have a value for excellence in everything you do on a practical level.
- Model God's character and nature every opportunity you get.
- Identify and remove challenges.
- Model the vision and share it with the body.

> *"My Lord, if I have now found favor in Your sight, do not pass on by Your servant."*
> — *Genesis 18:3*

Just as God is excellent in everything He does, we should have a value for excellence in everything we do on a practical level. We can help our members become excellent stewards in every aspect. Living a lifestyle of excellence on a practical level encompasses a person's resources, destiny, careful management of finances, avoidance of debt, etc.

On the corporate level, we need to run our churches in a way that doesn't overextend our resources—which isn't always easy to do because we are called to live by faith. We are people of faith who want to walk by faith even when God directs us to take a risk. Yes, there will be times when He asks us to leave "practical" living behind, but here is a good principle to keep in mind: To the extent that a word from the Lord violates sound counsel and the standard structures of administration, it is good to make sure you are actually hearing from Him. Get the word confirmed before you take that next step.

Think about it like this: In the Kingdom, we find rules and exceptions. The rule needs less guidance, while the exception needs more. In other words, we need *exceptional* guidance when we are seeking to "break the rules" and do exceptional things.

How to Build a Lifestyle of Excellence in Your Church

1. Raise up the vision.

Why is it important to have a vision for excellence? Because we want to model our Father's character and nature every opportunity we get! Pursuing excellence is one of the ways we do this. He has called us by His own excellence, as 2 Peter 1:3 says (NASB):

> *His divine power has granted to us everything pertaining to life and godliness, through the true knowledge of Him who called us by His own glory and excellence.*

2. Identify and remove challenges.

What do you value? How do you prioritize those values? Do your values and priorities line up with your calling as a church?

Look at how you manage your money, spend your time and allocate your talents; this will show you what your priorities really are. Does anything need to be adjusted in your personal life? In your church? As you are faithful to make those adjustments, you'll see a spirit of excellence begin to flourish.

3. Model your vision for excellence.

Incorporate the pursuit of excellence deeply into your own life. Take the time to do things well. Go before God and ask Him to show you what excellence looks like in your personal life. Everything you want to bring to your church has to be real inside of you before you can replicate it in others.

Preach on building a lifestyle of excellence, and encourage people to celebrate those who are organizing their lives well. Encourage excellence in every context, whether it is in people's homes, home groups, Sunday morning services, workplaces, government spheres or even at the grocery store. Highlight the people who are gifted administrators and those who are making adjustments in their lives so they can walk in a spirit of excellence.

6.4

Structures of Administrative Excellence

Focal point: We uncover what we need and work together for growth.

This focal point includes:

- Have ministries available that assist people in the administration of excellence.
- Find out what people need and offer classes in those areas.
- Seek to sow excellence into your structures.
- Have a system in place for raising up new expressions of administrative strength.

> *Do you not know that those who run in a race all run, but one receives the prize? Run in such a way that you may obtain it.*
> — *1 Corinthians 9:24*

In your congregation, do you have ministries available that assist individuals (and your church) in the administration of excellence? What do these ministries look like? What are they doing for people and how are they helping them? If you are unable to start your own ministry in a certain area, you could bring in outside ministries, speakers, teaching books or curricula that have similar DNA and use them in your congregation.

Here are a few ways you can build structures of excellence in your church:

1. Find out what people want to know and offer classes on those topics.

On a personal level, your church could offer adult classes that focus on issues like finances, time management and reaching your destiny. Query the congregation; find out the areas they feel they need to grow in and then make those classes available. Be sure each class includes enough time at the end for questions and answers.

Along with this, send leaders and overseers into the congregation just to ask people how they are. Build relationships on purpose, asking, "How can I serve you? What can I do to help you grow? Do you want to meet about this on a regular basis so I can support you?" These are good questions that need to be raised in our relationships with one another.

2. Seek to sow excellence into your structures.

On a corporate level, build the spirit of excellence into the structures that support your church. The church should be state-of-the-art in terms of media, music, sound systems, lighting, computer programs, applications, etc. Have the best programs in place with the most efficient use of resources, which produces the highest yield of quality, effectiveness and impact.

3. Raise up administrators.

Try to have a system in place for raising up new expressions of administrative strength. One way to do this is by addressing administration, both its importance and its calling, from the pulpit and seeing who responds. Who in your congregation has a heart for administration? Who is already moving in the spirit of excellence? Identify who they are, pray over them, develop and train them.

Create a developmental ladder in your church so administrative people can move into higher levels of leadership, administrative authority and oversight. This looks like creating entry-level admin roles, where people can demonstrate faithfulness without a tremendous amount of expertise, and midlevel administrative roles, which help people grow. Ultimately, these leaders-in-training are your candidates for deacons (workers or helpers) in your church.

Equip those who are uniquely called to administration, and help them raise up administrative sons and daughters. This will promote incredible expressions of excellence in your church.

6.5
Leadership of Administrative Excellence

Focal point: We effectively train, release and mentor new gifted administrators.

Steps to building administrative leadership:

- Identify
- Recruit (according to destiny)
- Train (on the job with supplementary classroom teaching)
- Deploy (transition them into their new roles with care)
- Support (monitor and nurture)

> *Therefore we also, since we are surrounded by so great a cloud of witnesses, let us lay aside every weight, and the sin which so easily ensnares us, and let us run with endurance the race that is set before us.*
> *— Hebrews 12:1*

The gift of administration is just as important to the health of the body as any other ministry. Look through your congregation and answer the following questions:

- Who walks in excellence in her occupation and how she serves other people?
- Who has revealed an aptitude for details and order?
- Who knows how to take something small, invest in it and produce an outcome that is far greater than his investment?

Identify these people and begin to speak to them about their gifts and potential.

For specific steps in how to produce leaders in your church or ministry, please refer to "Raising Up Leaders" in Section 1.5: Apostolic Leadership.

Theme 7
Kingdom Strategy

**We value supernatural strategic planning in
bringing God's purpose to pass.**

This theme includes:

- God's heart for strategic planning (Genesis 39; Jeremiah 29:11)
- We regularly and prayerfully plan and execute according to God's purpose.
- We regularly review why we exist and what we must do to fulfill our ministry.
- Our ministry goals are defined, measurable and attainable.
- Our ministry structures are flexible, effective and life giving.
- Our team is cohesive, united and suited to our ministry target group.

An Introduction to Strategic Planning

*The Lord was with Joseph, and he was a successful man; and he was in
the house of his master the Egyptian. And his master saw that the
Lord was with him and that the Lord made all he did to prosper in his
hand.*
— Genesis 39:2-3

In many ways, the story God is writing in your life is a mystery. He is *God*,
which means He is able to do exceedingly abundantly above all we ask or
think, and He is able to accomplish these things in a sequence all His own.
This means there will be seasons when things fall into place without your
help, and it seems like everything is working out on its own. You will look
around and realize that God is arranging the story and moving the pieces as
He sees fit. In these seasons, it is apparent that He has an agenda and
timeline, and He is in the mood to get things done.

But that is just a season. It doesn't always work that way.

God gave us logical minds and the ability to extrapolate, plan, set things in order and walk out goals and conditions. Scripture tells us to run our races well:

> *Do you not know that those who run in a race all run, but one receives the prize? Run in such a way that you may obtain it.*
> — *1 Corinthians 9:24*

> *Let us run with endurance the race that is set before us.*
> — *Hebrews 12:1*

Apart from God *commandeering* our efforts and taking us a whole other direction, it is always wise to have a plan with goals and objectives in mind.

Goals are large outcomes—the end result, the distant target. Objectives, meanwhile, are sub-goals that allow you to achieve outcomes in a carefully executed manner. In football terms, the primary "goal" is winning the game. The objectives are a series of points scored through touchdowns and field goals.

Corporately speaking, many goals and objectives are practical considerations: "What kind of resources do we need? How much money do we need? What kind of facility?" Obtaining those resources could be a set of objectives. Another set of objectives is uncovered as we answer these questions: "What kind of team do we need to accomplish our goal? How long will it take to build that team, and how are we going to build it? What are the different steps and stages of building?"

Each of your goals needs to be broken down into large-to-small sequences that can be prioritized and implemented. If your vision is to secure a building, for example, a set of reasonable factors comes into play: First, you need to start looking for a building and contract a realtor. You need to figure out the necessary square footage and how much money you have available to finish out the building. Those are reasonable steps that enable you to move forward.

Define the things you want to accomplish: Win the game. Lead at halftime. Have great team dynamics. Grow the church. Raise up leaders. Reach the lost.

Pay the bills. Once you understand where you're going and the commitment it will take to get there, it becomes relatively simple to set things in order.

The Kingdom Plan

Every prophetic environment has five general Kingdom goals:

1. Receive vision from the Lord and communicate it to your congregation.
2. Build the vision, and build your leaders and congregation.
3. Reach the lost.
4. Create connection and community.
5. Communicate truth in a transformational way.

Those are our primary goals, and from these goals, individual churches build objectives that are more specific to their calling and region.

7.1
Vision for Kingdom Strategy

Focal point: We regularly and prayerfully plan and execute according to God's purpose.

This focal point includes:

- Just as Jesus is a strategic thinker, we are called to be strategic thinkers.
- Seek God for His vision.
- Keep the vision in front of the people.
- Make sure your values and priorities match your vision.
- Build programs and ministries that coincide with the vision.

Now to Him who is able to do exceedingly abundantly above all that we ask or think, according to the power that works in us, to Him be glory in the church by Christ Jesus to all generations, forever and ever. Amen.
— *Ephesians 3:20-21*

God likes to plan. He sees the end from the beginning and works all things according to the counsel of His will (Ephesians 1:11). He is outside of time— interacting with all time, at the same time, in His eternal timeframe. Therefore, He is able to move us forward with a degree of intention and yet still allow us to be free moral agents, who are able to participate or not participate according to our willingness to choose His grace. Just as He is a strategic thinker, we are called to be strategic thinkers.

Here are a few ways you can begin to implement an overall strategy and plan in your church:

1. Seek God for His vision.

The first step in any planning process is to seek God for His plans. On a regular basis, come before Him and pray, "What is Your heart? What is Your passion and purpose right now? How can we more effectively align our church with what matters to You?"

Once or twice a year, gather with your team for a day or overnight retreat. Spend time in worship and prayer, and seek the Lord, praying, "We are not here to build a church or fulfill our own plans. We want to fulfill *Your* vision. We invite You to download more of Your vision to us." You can come away from these times with a much greater clarity of God's purpose and plans for you.

2. Keep the vision in front of the people.

Consistently give your people a fresh sense of God's purpose for the church. Consider the following questions:

- Why are you gathering together like this?
- Why do you worship?
- Why do you spend time in the Word and reach out to the poor?
- Why do you share your faith with your friends?

Weave your vision into different teachings, and encourage other members of your team to present it as well.

Vision gives pain a purpose. You're asking people to sacrifice and calling them to a lifestyle and commitment that will cause them to step outside their comfort zones. You're calling them to a high level of service, and to reach that level of service, they need a *purpose* that will help make sense of their pain and sacrifice.

3. Make sure your values and priorities match your vision.

How you're allocating your time, energy and money need to be in line with where you want to lead the church.

Many churches say, "Our job is to make disciples," but their priorities don't align with that vision. How much of their time, energy and money is actually going toward that end? Ultimately, you have to step back and say, "If our job is to make disciples, then we should be putting the majority of our time, energy and money into reaching people." Start evaluating in this manner and change your church's "ecosystem" to match the vision you know God has for you.

4. Build programs and ministries that coincide with the vision.

Start pointing your time, energy and various ministries toward what God has told you to do. Work with your leaders in this process, because you depend on them to disseminate the priorities and programs that will move your church forward.

It is important that all members of your leadership team own the vision and how God is moving in your church. This allows them to really represent you as they go into the congregation and lead various ministries. As these things occur, the people will move into a thriving experience of Kingdom community that will bring transformation to your church and the city around you.

7.2

Culture of Kingdom Strategy

**Focal point: We regularly review why we exist and
what we must do to fulfill our ministry.**

This focal point includes:

- Jesus had a target while on the earth, and so do we.
- As a church, define your target and know who you are called to reach.
- Know your team in light of your target.
- Understand your values and priorities.

> *For I know the thoughts that I think toward you, says the Lord, thoughts of peace and not of evil, to give you a future and a hope.*
> *— Jeremiah 29:11*

Jesus had a very specific target group when He was on the earth. He declared, "I came for the lost sheep of Israel." Obviously, God had a plan in place for the rest of the world; He knew He would be sending Paul to the nations a few years later. But Jesus' primary target was clear, and He consistently remained focused on that target.

Similarly, God has a target for each of us. Let's look at how we can stay focused and keep our eyes on that target.

1. What is your target?

What is your bulls-eye as a church? Why are you in your city? What has God called you to do? What is the target you are moving toward?

Divine focus is like a dartboard. You have your bulls-eye in the middle, followed by ever-increasing concentric rings that help you determine how close you are to the main goal God has for you.

As a church, define your target. Know who you are called to reach. This is not an effort to exclude people, but it allows you to make things blessedly simple: "This is who we are. This is who we're called to reach. They are our target—and then beyond them, we can reach and serve other people as well."

2. Know your team in light of your target.

Your team needs to be suited to your target group. For example, if you're trying to reach senior citizens but your team is made up of 20-year-olds—that could be a little challenging. If you're trying to reach Cambodian refugees but your team is made up of suburban white kids, that might be more difficult than if you had a team of Cambodians.

The simple truth is that you will be most able to reach the people you are most like. That was why Jesus came as a Jew and not a Babylonian or Roman—because He was assigned to reach the Jews. That was why Paul grew up in Damascus and was part of a larger subset of Roman citizenship— because he was called to reach beyond the confines of Israel. Not every team member needs to be exactly like the people you're reaching, but cross-cultural ministry requires more intentionality in the process.

3. Understand your values and priorities.

Do your values line up with those of the target you're called to reach? For example, Western culture values authenticity, integrity and intentionality. Those are key things in our culture today, and in order to reach our culture, we have to understand those values. Consider your values and how they match the values of your target.

Also, consider your priorities and how you're "spending" your time, energy and money. Be sure your priorities match your vision, because your actions as a church prove what is really important to you. Begin to adapt your church's calendar, lifestyle and focus so everything lines up with your vision.

As you begin to think more intentionally about your values, priorities, team and target, you will find yourself with a growing, thriving church that powerfully brings transformation to your region.

7.3
Lifestyle of Kingdom Strategy

Focal point: Our ministry goals are defined, measurable and attainable.

This focal point includes:

- God encourages us to plan according to His plan.
- Make your goals well defined, rational and measurable.
- Every church needs to be in a circular process of achievement, reevaluation and achievement again in order to fulfill the mission.
- Make your goals attainable.

> *But He said to them, "I must preach the kingdom of God to the other cities also, because for this purpose I have been sent."*
> — *Luke 4:43*

As an intensely purposeful Being, God has a plan, and He encourages us to plan according to His plan, while remembering that we are completely dependent upon Him. We need to work in partnership with Him to accomplish the purposes He ordained for us.

A *vision* is what you see.
A *mission* is what you do to accomplish what you see.
A mission without goals is just an idea.

We need to set goals and objectives and accomplish them, but these things need to be placed before the Lord, with a sense of dependence upon Him.

Also, our goals need to be realistic. Many of us have probably heard pastors and other leaders declare, "We want 1000 people by two months!" But they were starting with a group of 60. God could do that, yes…but without a plan in place, the chances of achieving such a goal are slim. To accomplish a massive goal, you need to have a good plan.

Here are a few tips for setting goals:

1. Make your goals well defined.

You and your leadership team can set up goals in a way that is friendly, inclusive and fun. Make sure your goals are rational and well defined:

- What are you going after?
- What is your desired outcome?
- How do you define this intended outcome in terms of quality and magnitude?

2. Make your goals measurable.

It is easy to measure "outward" things, like how much money you brought in and how many people visit the church on a Sunday. However, the inward, *qualitative* measurements are the ones you want the most. How many people are developing into maturity? How many leaders are taking on new leadership in your church?

Don't be afraid of measurement…and don't be afraid of readjusting the plan if necessary. Ultimately, every church needs to be in a circular process of achievement, reevaluation and achievement again in order to fulfill what God has put on their hearts to do.

3. Make your goals attainable.

Nothing is worse than setting a goal too high and then falling short. This damages your church's momentum and enthusiasm. Instead, set and achieve smaller and more measurable goals to bring forth the quality of church you long to see. Momentum is a factor of many little successes that will work to increase your velocity, so your church can accomplish the bigger things God has for you.

7.4
Structures of Kingdom Strategy

Focal point: Our ministry structures are flexible, effective and life giving.

This focal point includes:

- Build structures that are consistent with God's plan and are also effective in terms of reaching the people around you.
- Your structures need to be intentional, goal oriented and life giving.
- Instead of being burdens, programs should be servants to the people who are carrying them.

> *So it was, from the time that he had made him overseer of his house and all that he had, that the Lord blessed the Egyptian's house for Joseph's sake; and the blessing of the Lord was on all that he had in the house and in the field.*
> *— Genesis 39:5*

God has invited you to partner with Him, fulfilling His intention for the city He has assigned to you and the people He has given you to lead. When you know His intentions and His overall plan, you can build structures that are consistent with His plan and are effective in terms of reaching the people around you.

Structures (programs and ministries within your church) help channel your church in the right direction. Your people especially need these structures because they aren't exposed to the vision as much as you are. As the leader, you know the plan well because you're around it 24 hours a day. You're thinking about intentionality and how to move forward, but your average member is getting only two to three hours of exposure to you a week. With the right structures in place, you can lead people more effectively, and they can find a sense of fulfillment in the vision they are following with you.

Here are a few ways you can build structures that will produce the kind of growth you're looking for:

1. Your structures need to be intentional.

The programs and ministries in your church need to match your purpose as a church. What is your church called to do? Who are you called to reach? What is the "nature" of the city you're in, and what are the ramifications of your target? Remember why you are here, and be intentional about following God's plan for you as a church.

2. Your structures need to be goal-oriented.

Much of our church culture is not very goal-oriented. We tend to be fairly relaxed about achievement, so we often join ministries, are a part of the team for a few months or years, and eventually leave without accomplishing anything important.

Build a culture of intentionality in your church, so people know what they want to achieve and when. When this culture is in place, you can produce within people the momentum and fruit that validates their sacrifice. You are asking for their time, money, energy and talent—give them results that will validate their efforts.

3. Your structures need to be life-giving.

Programs should not be burdens; they should be servants to the people who are carrying them. When Jesus referred to the Sabbath, He said, "People weren't made for the Sabbath. Sabbath was made for people." The same is true with ministries, structures and programs.

One mistake churches often make is trying to keep old programs alive. At times we blister our hands as we shovel "coal" into the program to keep it burning…when the program died a year ago and needs to be given a gracious, respectful burial. A group shouldn't be kept going if it has outlived its usefulness.

What is God doing in your church? What does He want to do in your church? Find what gives you life. As programs were made for people, be sure they serve people effectively.

So in summary, build healthy structures that are intentional, goal-oriented and life-giving. In this way, they will produce the kind of thriving congregation you desire, which will in turn produce the kind of impact you want to have in your community.

7.5
Kingdom Strategy Leadership

**Focal point: Our team is cohesive, united and
suited to our ministry target group.**

Steps to building strategic leadership:

- Identify
- Recruit (according to destiny)
- Train (on the job with supplementary classroom teaching)
- Deploy (transition them into their new roles with care)
- Support (monitor and nurture)

> *The keeper of the prison did not look into anything that was under
> Joseph's authority, because the Lord was with him; and whatever he
> did, the Lord made it prosper.*
> — *Genesis 39:23*

God's Word says that the horse is prepared for battle, but the victory is the
Lord's. In other words, we do our part and God does His.

The book of Proverbs speaks again and again about the power of planning
and wise counsel. Strategically minded people are like weapons in the hand of
a general. Theory alone won't get us far—we need strategy and structure to
carry us toward our goals.

- Who in your church is an excellent strategist?
- Who is gifted in hearing God's voice in specific areas like finances or
  time management?
- When you preach on Kingdom strategy, who responds?

Begin to meet with these people on a regular basis. Pray with them and see
how God might want to use them to build up the church and touch your
community.

For specific steps in how to produce leaders in your church or ministry, please refer to "Raising Up Leaders" in Section 1.5: Apostolic Leadership.

Theme 8
Kingdom Servanthood

We value biblical servanthood as an expression of Kingdom ministry.

This theme includes:

- God's heart for servanthood (Isaiah 53; John 13; Philippians 2)
- Every member of our church embraces the call to serve others.
- Our church provides many and varied service opportunities.
- Our members serve each other in times of crisis and need.
- We provide care and support systems for those who serve.
- We recognize servant leaders and release them into new levels of service.

An Introduction to Servanthood

This is a shocking concept when you think about it at length, but God is the Creator of all things—and yet servanthood is a deep, intimate part of His heart. Jesus reiterated this idea again and again:

> *"He who is greatest among you shall be your servant."*
> *— Matthew 23:11*

> *"Blessed are those servants whom the master, when he comes, will find watching. Assuredly, I say to you that he will gird himself and have them sit down to eat, and will come and serve them."*
> *— Luke 12:37*

> *"I am among you as the One who serves."*
> *— Luke 22:27*

When we demonstrate Jesus in practical ways by serving other people, not only do we make a difference in their immediate lives, but we also gain the right to lead them.

The world will listen to a person who is a true servant.

In John 13 when Jesus was with His friends in the upper room, He humbled Himself and washed their feet. Scripture indicates that His ability to model servanthood was based in His absolute security in His identity. Jesus knew "that the Father had given all things into His hands, and that He had come from God and was going to God" (verse 3). Later in verse 14 He said, "If I then, your Lord and Teacher, have washed your feet, you also ought to wash one another's feet." Servanthood is the foundation for all leadership and influence; servanthood and leadership are two sides of the same coin. As Bill Johnson, senior leader of Bethel Church in Redding, California, says, "Rule with the heart of a servant. Serve with the heart of a king."

Paul also made the servant heart of God very clear:

> *Let this mind be in you which was also in Christ Jesus, who, being in the form of God, did not consider it robbery to be equal with God, but made Himself of no reputation, taking the form of a bondservant, and coming in the likeness of men.*
> — *Philippians 2:6-7*

Jesus emptied Himself to be a servant. He is a servant God. Servanthood is the basis of all true leadership.

Different Types and Times of Servanthood

Administration and deaconal ministry are two different things. *Administration* involves looking after resources, the calendar, facility, finances and technical and media issues.

Deaconal ministry, on the other hand, refers to the various servant aspects of the church. This is anything that falls within the practical care of its members: greeting and ushering, running a coffee house or bookstore and any other ministry that provides services for the people. Deaconal ministry is sometimes called *non-people ministry* because it oversees people's practical needs.

We see deaconal leaders in Luke 8, where women looked after Jesus' practical needs. Later in the book of Acts, deaconal ministry becomes much clearer when seven men were appointed to see to widows' needs. As a side note, it is interesting that several of the "deacons" in this passage eventually ended up moving into other powerful ministries. One became an evangelist, and another was Stephen, who some people believe became a prophet, based on the defense he gave just before his death.

The point is that some people are called to serve the church long term and become senior deacons or workers in the Body of Christ. Others, meanwhile, are called to serve as deacons only for a season as they develop into their full ministries.

A quick note about serving: Unfortunately, many people serve out of duty when there's a higher motivation: *delight*. Though honorable, duty isn't a sustainable long-term motivator, but if you can find the pleasure of God in the midst of serving others, you can go on to transform the world.

8.1
Vision for Servanthood

**Focal point: Every member of our church
embraces the call to serve others.**

This focal point includes:

- Servanthood should be the heart that drives us as we go out to change the world.
- Servanthood opens the door to leadership.
- Make the vision practical and model it for others.
- Make the vision for servanthood a priority in your leadership team and church.

  Let a man so consider us, as servants of Christ and stewards of the mysteries of God.
  — 1 Corinthians 4:1

Servanthood should be the heart that drives us as we go out to change the world. It is the combination of activity and humility; we see the good that ought to be done, and so we activate ourselves to serve with hearts of genuine love and compassion. Unfortunately, the Church has built a reputation for having the opposite spirit. Some of us haven't served in humility and gentleness; instead, we rode in like bosses and tried to rule people and legislate morality over them.

**The Church has lost the right to lead
because we have lost the will to serve.**

Until we are willing to serve the poor and ungodly, the just and the unjust, those who are unrighteous along with the righteous, we have no right to expect to be heard. Servanthood opens the door to leadership.

How to Build a Vision for Servanthood in Your Church

1. Make the vision practical.

The concept of serving others doesn't have to be hard. We can think about it in simple ways. We find servanthood in the very heart of God. Having embraced the form of a servant, Jesus told the disciples, "I am among you as the One who serves" (Luke 22:27). Even many of the prophecies about Jesus in the Old Testament refer to Him as the "suffering servant." Philippians 2 encourages us to have the same mind as Christ, who became the servant of all.

Servanthood is an act of love that is deeply embedded in God's heart. He is the One who sees to our needs and provides for us. That is where the vision to serve comes from—the heart of God. If we want to be leaders in the world, we need to be the servants of all (Mark 9:35). Think about what that means for you and your church.

2. Model your vision for servanthood.

Practice being a servant in simple, everyday ways. Consider these questions with your team: Why is it important to be a servant? How will people come to know God better as they serve others?

Be careful not to instill within yourself a sense of legalism when it comes to serving. Joy is a much better motivator, one with a phenomenal amount of power. You can motivate people for a season with duty—or you can motivate them for a lifetime with joy. Discover the delight aspect of serving others and then spread that delight to your leadership team.

3. Make the vision for servanthood a priority.

We are all servants of the Lord doing our part. When the day is done, the pay's the same—we all get to go be with Him. Equip your church to be servants, both to one another and your city. Spend time preaching about servanthood and how it functions in the Body of Christ. This is not manipulation or an attempt to *compel* people to help out; it is insight into the servant heart of God and how He called us to serve as He serves.

Celebrate acts of servanthood in your core leadership group so your vision for servanthood naturally extends to the rest of the church. As people see the importance of servanthood, they will begin to adopt it as a value in their own lives.

8.2

Culture of Servanthood

**Focal point: Our church provides many
and varied service opportunities.**

This focal point includes:

- Your culture as a church is who you are.
- Building culture is the first step in moving from vision to reality.
- Personify the culture yourself, and infuse it into your primary team and congregation.
- Consider "tithing" your time to God.

> *The Lord redeems the soul of His servants,*
> *And none of those who trust in Him shall be condemned.*
> — *Psalm 34:22*

All ministry boils down to serving God and people with a true servant's heart. That heart did not begin in us; it began in Jesus. He is the ultimate servant leader. Therefore, our goal as servant leaders is to create a whole congregation of servant leaders who fulfill God's purposes on the earth.

Remember, *culture* is the shared values, priorities and practices, along with the traditions, symbols and expressions, that unite a community. Your culture reflects who your church is at a deep level. As you clarify your values, you establish your priorities—things that are more or less important for how you spend your time, energy and resources. Out of your priorities emerge your everyday practices (things you naturally do on a day-to-day basis). Each of these individual "steps" works to establish a culture of servanthood in your church.

Here are a few other things to consider as you build your church culture:

1. As a leader, personify the culture yourself.

To create a servant culture in your church, discuss with your leadership team the key values that support a servant culture. Model the lifestyle you want to create, and then provide ongoing opportunities for people to serve.

The servant heart needs to be made visible on multiple levels from the core of the church outward. There is no such thing as the high and mighty; we never reach a spiritual level where we are no longer called to serve. The congregation needs to see their leaders being servants—doing things like picking up the paper in the hallway, cleaning bathrooms, taking meals to sick people, etc. A true culture of servanthood begins at the core and spreads outward. The leadership team—the senior pastor, spouse and core team members—need to model what true service looks like.

2. Infuse that culture into your primary team and congregation.

Preach about servanthood and talk about how we serve the Lord and one another through our generosity, sacrifice and willingness to commit to others. Some churches have two services on Sunday mornings, and it has little to do with overcrowding; they just want to create more opportunities for volunteers and activate more people to serve. Give people a variety of ways and opportunities to serve.

3. Train your people to dedicate concentrated time to God.

Scripture isn't clear about what God "requires" from us regarding our time. Jesus said, "I want everything. I want all your time. I want all your energy. I want all your money." But devoting every minute of the day to pursuing spiritual reality isn't a sustainable lifestyle, so what are we to do? One possibility is tithing our time.

Just as the principle of tithing our income is not a "law" (an action required for salvation), the idea of *tithing your time* is not meant to be legalistic or "religious." It is simply interesting to think about. There are 168 hours in the week, and about 50-60 of those hours are spent sleeping or in personal hygiene, which leaves us 110-112 hours. If you were to "tithe" the remaining time, it would mean committing 10-12 hours a week to serving Jesus in a concentrated way. This works out to be three or four commitments a week that are specifically Kingdom oriented. When you break it down, it really isn't hard to fill that time slot.

8.3
Lifestyle of Servanthood

Focal point: Our members serve each other in times of crisis and need.

This focal point includes:

- Model your vision for servanthood.
- Identify and remove challenges, and examine your values and priorities.
- Spread the vision through your church.
- Help people build servanthood into their lifestyles by offering volunteer opportunities in areas of servanthood and leadership.

> *Let them say continually,*
> *"Let the Lord be magnified,*
> *Who has pleasure in the prosperity of His servant."*
> *— Psalm 35:27*

Whatever values you embrace as a church will gradually become a way of life for you. You'll notice that a set of practices begins to emerge that reflects the things your church does naturally. The people don't do these things because they are told to do them or even because you have programs set up to help them do them. Instead, they do them because these are elements deeply entrenched in their hearts as a community.

How to Build a Lifestyle of Servanthood in Your Church

1. Model your vision for servanthood.

What is your vision for servanthood? At its core, true servanthood means having a heart that mirrors the heart of God. We love and serve one another because He does these things. Jesus said, "It is enough for a disciple that he be like his teacher, and a servant like his master" (Matthew 10:25).

Make servanthood personal. Incorporate it deeply into your own life, and build it into your family's lifestyle. Remember, everything you want to bring to your church has to be real inside of you before you can replicate it in others.

2. Identify and remove challenges.

As a leader, how do you "prove" the values of your church? By realizing where your priorities lie. You reveal your priorities in how you allocate time, energy, money and talent. You naturally distribute your resources in order of preference and importance. If a church says, "We really value community," but their calendar does not reflect that value, they have other priorities that are stronger. They believe community is a priority to them and *want* it to be a priority, but it really isn't a priority.

Examine your values and priorities. What do you truly value? Are you giving your best for the purposes God created for you? Are you doing so in a balanced way that is sustainable over the long haul?

As a leader, does anything need to be adjusted in your life or in your church? Begin to make those adjustments.

3. Spread the vision through your church.

Preach on building a lifestyle of servanthood, and encourage people to take note of those who are trying to live as Jesus would, with a serving heart.

Help people build servanthood into their lifestyles by offering volunteer opportunities in areas of servanthood and leadership. No matter your church's size or background, every congregation has a wide spectrum for service: elders, worship leaders, greeters and ushers, janitors and other cleaners, parking attendants, nursery and children's church ministers, etc.

You could even build volunteering into your church membership structure. For instance, you could encourage new members to fill a servant role within the church for six months. Not only would this help to undergird the church, but it would also help your members learn about servanthood and build it naturally as a lifestyle. Celebrate acts of service in your church, both the "large" acts and those that seem simple and basic.

8.4
Structures of Servanthood

Focal point: We provide care and support systems for those who serve.

This focal point includes:

- We never reach a spiritual level where we are no longer called to serve.
- Model servanthood as a leader.
- Raise up servant leaders; put out calls and see who responds.
- Train your servant leaders to raise up teams of servants.

> *Let Your work appear to Your servants,*
> *And Your glory to their children.*
> *— Psalm 90:16*

If Jesus Himself came as a servant (Philippians 2:7), what does that mean for us? We never reach some lofty spiritual level where we are no longer called to serve.

How do you build servant ministries within your church?

1. Model servanthood as a leader.

The first step in building structures of servanthood in your church is making the servant heart visible on multiple levels within the church, from the core outward. Begin by letting the church see how important servanthood is to you personally. Model what true service looks like.

The congregation needs to see its leaders being servants. When the church sees how much you value servanthood, it will open their hearts to respond in a similar manner.

2. Raise up servant leaders.

Building servant ministries has a lot to do with the servant leaders you are raising up—men and women who have the gift of servanthood evident in their spiritual gift-mix. One way to discover these people is to present your church with opportunities to serve and see who responds. Pull these people aside, pray with them and put together a core servant team. These people will be your deacons and can help oversee and run the church so it will have greater health and impact.

If you are able to have multiple teams for each kind of ministry your church offers (more than one team of greeters, ushers, children's church workers, etc.), you can give people the chance to serve by rotating teams.

3. Train your servant leaders to raise up other servants.

Create opportunities for growth at deeper levels of servanthood for those who are called to serve in the church life-long—that is, it is their passion to serve the body long term and they are wired for it. In the concentric model of church leadership, people can grow in the servant calling. A person can move from being just a helper who shows up and provides support on a regular basis to being part of a servant team, which is the next "level" of servanthood with a greater commitment. She could then develop to the next level—that of being a servant leader—and she could eventually become a servant overseer: a head worker or deacon who oversees four or five servant ministries.

It is vital that people who are called to servant ministry within the church are able to serve on a wide level. Help them grow and prepare them to raise up other servants in a way that displays the care and heart of Jesus.

8.5
Servant Leadership

**Focal point: We recognize servant leaders and
release them into new levels of service.**

Steps to building servant leadership:

- Identify
- Recruit (according to destiny)
- Train (on the job with supplementary classroom teaching)
- Deploy (transition them into their new roles with care)
- Support (monitor and nurture)

> *Your servant meditates on Your statutes.*
> *— Psalm 119:23*

Who is wired to serve in your church? There are a few different ways to discover these people. Here are some ideas:

- Preach about servanthood and see who responds.
- Use a gift assessment tool like the one we have at www.DestinyFinder.com to get a better idea of people's gifts and callings.
- Know what to look for. People gifted in servanthood usually are able to connect well with others; they are executors who know how to make decisions. Within their spiritual gift-mix (Romans 12), they are motivated by mercy, giving and serving.

Currently, there is a tremendous opportunity for the servant office to be awakened in the Body of Christ. The more we emphasize it and raise up leaders who walk in humility and with a servant's heart, the more fruit we will see in this area.

For specific steps in how to produce leaders in your church or ministry, please refer to "Raising Up Leaders" in Section 1.5: Apostolic Leadership.

Theme 9
Healing Ministry

We value healing and deliverance as an expression of God's purpose.

This theme includes:

- God's heart for healing (Isaiah 61; Matthew 8:2-3)
- We provide specialty small groups with various healing emphases.
- We train peer counselors and provide inner healing for the brokenhearted.
- We provide trained ministers to pray for physical healing.
- We provide or recommend trusted professional counselors to our people.
- We provide specialized ministry to free people from spiritual bondage.

An Introduction to the Hospital:
The Healing Center in the Church

"The Spirit of the Lord God is upon Me,
Because the Lord has anointed Me
To preach good tidings to the poor;
He has sent Me to heal the brokenhearted,
To proclaim liberty to the captives,
And the opening of the prison to those who are bound;
To proclaim the acceptable year of the Lord."
— *Isaiah 61:1-2*

Isaiah 61 holds an amazing Messianic prophecy that Jesus, the fulfillment of the prophecy, declared at the beginning of His ministry. What was the core message of this prophecy? That God loves the broken.

Isaiah 61 is a key description of Jesus' ministry
to the Church.

As His representatives, we need to be as concerned about people's hearts as He is and equip ourselves to care for and help lead the broken into ever-increasing healing and restoration.

God the Comforter

The world may be in rough shape today, but it didn't start out that way. In the beginning, God declared that His creation was "good." After He created humanity, those made in His image, He even said, "It is very good."

Brokenness came to our planet as a result of sin. The enemy's work released a terrible legacy of sin and brokenness in people's lives, but that isn't the end of the story. The vision for healing is embedded in the very heart of God.

**As we grow to become more and more like Jesus,
we naturally begin to adopt His vision for healing as well.
It becomes rooted in our hearts.**

Healing is the gifts of mercy and compassion at work. Paul wrote in 2 Corinthians 1:3-4, "Blessed be the God and Father of our Lord Jesus Christ, the Father of mercies and God of all comfort, who comforts us in all our tribulation." That is where healing begins—in the comforting process. We are comforted by the One who made us, and as that happens, we are equipped to comfort others with the comfort we received from God.

The goal of healing ministry is to provide a way for the broken and hurting to encounter God's healing and comfort, so they find relief and restoration in their lives. Every church needs to offer healing ministry of some sort and seek to impact people at greater and greater levels in a holistic way, helping them overcome the challenges of life and move forward.

Healing ministries commonly found in prophetic environments include healing rooms (where teams of people pray for the sick for physical healing), inner healing and professional counseling services.

*"Comfort, yes, comfort My people!"
Says your God.
"Speak comfort to Jerusalem, and cry out to her,
That her warfare is ended,*

That her iniquity is pardoned."
— *Isaiah 40:1-2*

9.1
Vision for Healing Ministry

**Focal point: We provide specialty small groups
with various healing emphases.**

This focal point includes:

- Help people see their own hearts and their need for God's comfort.
- Remember your authority in Christ.
- Make healing a priority in your church.

> *He will feed His flock like a shepherd;*
> *He will gather the lambs with His arm,*
> *And carry them in His bosom,*
> *And gently lead those who are with young.*
> — *Isaiah 40:11*

God is a Father and a Shepherd, and it is His kindness that leads us to repentance (Romans 2:4). David even wrote, "Your right hand has held me up, Your gentleness has made me great" (Psalm 18:35).

How can you promote a vision for love and healing in your congregation, so people develop a passion for the healing and comfort of God?

1. Help people see their own hearts and their need for God's comfort.

People need to be introduced to the Father's heart. Comfort is a critical part of any vision for healing, and it is found in the heart of the Father. Help people find their way into right relationship with Him.

Not every person is in tune with what is going on in his heart. It is important to help people understand their pain, brokenness and need for forgiveness. When necessary, gently challenge what people are thinking and lovingly show them how they can learn to think more wisely, based on the truth of Scripture.

2. Remember your authority in Christ.

Any time we discuss a vision for healing, we have to remember our authority in Christ to release healing. Take steps to recognize and learn the authority you have, so you can do what Jesus did. Scripture says He did good things and healed all those who were oppressed by the devil. That is our calling as well.

3. Make healing a priority in your congregation.

Preach about healing and equip your church to pray for others for healing. Promote the vision for healing on a regular basis and keep declaring, "This is who we are. This is where we're going. This is the kind of love we want to express to others." This will help your people commit themselves to the vision and exemplify it in their lives.

Who in your church has experienced God's healing? Bring them to the front and have them share their testimonies. Celebrate healing, even if it seems small, and get people excited to see God move in this way.

9.2
Culture of Healing

**Focal point: We train peer counselors and provide
inner-healing for the brokenhearted.**

This focal point includes:

- *Culture* is the shared values, priorities and practices that unite a community.
- Personify the culture yourself.
- Make mercy available; pray for the sick and wounded in every one of your meetings.
- Infuse your vision into your primary team and bring it to the church.

  And behold, a leper came and worshiped Him, saying, "Lord, if You are willing, You can make me clean."

  Then Jesus put out His hand and touched him, saying, "I am willing; be cleansed." Immediately his leprosy was cleansed.
  — Matthew 8:2-3

The recorded words of Jesus will change our lives, yet it is important to remember He did more than speak! When we talk about His *words*, we also need to talk about His *works*. The words and works of Jesus form the gospel—they are the good news.

As a leader, try to build a culture that thrives on both the raw words of the gospel as well as the power of the Lord found in healing.

Remember, *culture* is the shared values, priorities and practices, along with the traditions, symbols and expressions, that unite a community. Your culture reflects who your church is at a deep level. As you clarify your values, you establish your priorities—things that are more or less important for how you spend your time, energy and resources. Out of your priorities emerge your everyday practices (things you naturally do on a day-to-day basis). Each of these individual "steps" works to establish a culture of healing in your church.

Here are a few other things to consider as you build your church culture:

1. As a leader, personify the culture yourself.

As John Wimber said, culture is best built from the inside out. If you want to build something, start in the leader; then move on to the team and finally the congregation. Give your people a vision and infuse them with the values and priorities that will help them become good developers of the vision in their own right.

What values, priorities and practices form the foundation of a culture of healing? Primarily, a culture of healing is kind and safe. Members of the congregation know they don't have to perform or be perfect. They are permitted to struggle and be vulnerable, and they understand they won't be removed from the family if they are less than "put together." Your church culture needs to give people permission to be in process.

A culture of healing also offers grace, opportunities for transformation and trust that honors confidentiality. It avoids gossip and, again, doesn't penalize its members for their less-than-perfect moments.

2. Make mercy available.

In every meeting, pray for the sick and wounded. Prayer should be a main component of your home groups, and all your leaders should be trained to pray for the sick, even if healing is not their primary gifting.

Talk about healing with your team, and make certain to share testimonies of healing. *Show* people what a culture of healing can look like.

3. Infuse your vision into your primary team and bring it to the church.

Promote your vision for healing on a regular basis and celebrate it well. A culture of healing thrives when its individual members discover who they are in Christ and are empowered and equipped to impact the world around them, both in the church and outside of it. Our calling is to do the same things Jesus did, and He healed "all who were oppressed by the devil" (Acts 10:38).

9.3
Lifestyle of Healing

Focal point: We provide trained ministers to pray for physical healing.

This focal point includes:

- Living a lifestyle of healing looks like connecting to the heartbeat of God, who loves the broken.
- Identify and remove any internal challenges to loving others.
- Give people the opportunity to learn about healing and to develop the necessary skills to live a healing lifestyle.

> *"A bruised reed He will not break,*
> *And smoking flax He will not quench."*
> *— Isaiah 42:3*

What does it mean to live a lifestyle of healing? In simple terms, it means we connect with the heartbeat of God, who loves the broken and downtrodden; He isn't willing even to damage a bruised reed. Mercy and healing can be so embedded in a church that God's people become known as people of love.

How to Build a Lifestyle of Healing in Your Church

1. Promote your vision for healing.

> *"But to you who fear My name*
> *The Sun of Righteousness shall arise*
> *With healing in His wings."*
> *— Malachi 4:2*

A lifestyle of healing means we have a consistent value for healing that is seen everywhere within the church, from the core leadership team to the youngest child attending Sunday school. We pray for the sick in the supermarket line and on Sunday mornings.

**Essentially, living a lifestyle of healing means
we know how to love well.**

When we see people at church who look downcast, we ask them how they are
doing and it isn't a rhetorical question—we ask because we care. We want
deep connection with others and to bring healing to them.

2. Identify and remove any internal challenges to loving others.

How would you answer the following questions?

- How does your church do when it comes to loving others?
- Do you feel like your church loves others the way Jesus loves them?
- How does your church treat "sinners"?
- When new people come to your church, do they feel loved and accepted?

Our actions prove our values. It's one thing to say we love others, but it's
another thing altogether to *show* we love others. To know what we actually
value, we have to look at how we manage our money, spend our time and
assign our talents. These things "prove" what is truly important to us and our
churches.

Does anything need to be adjusted in your church so your congregation loves
people the way Jesus does?

3. Share your vision with the body and give them the opportunity to learn.

Give people the opportunity to learn about healing and to develop the
necessary skills to live a healing lifestyle. You can begin to do this by
preaching about healing from the pulpit on a regular basis, hosting
conferences on healing, bringing in special speakers, etc. In every way, show
people what a lifestyle of healing could look like.

9.4

Structures of Healing

Focal point: We provide or recommend trusted professional counselors to our people.

This focal point includes:

- One of the key roles of every church is to provide different kinds of healing opportunities for its members.
- Train your leaders in healing.
- Maintain a victorious perspective.
- Promote your vision for healing on a regular basis.

> *"I have seen his ways, and will heal him;*
> *I will also lead him,*
> *And restore comforts to him*
> *And to his mourners."*
> *— Isaiah 57:18*

A key role of every church is to provide different kinds of healing opportunities for its members. Some churches create counseling centers; some have specialty small groups that deal with certain kinds of past hurts or addictive behaviors. Some have group healing rooms or ministries dedicated to inner healing. If you don't have these ministries in place, we encourage you to build the programs and ministries your church needs to walk in deeper healing.

Depending on the size of your church and how many healing ministries you have in place, you may want to appoint a leader over this branch of the church to help foster the growth of additional healing ministries, as well as ministers who know how to facilitate healing.

Here are a few things to think about as you build up your church's healing ministries:

1. Train your leaders in healing.

Who in your leadership and congregation is gifted in this area of healing and mercy? Make it possible for these people to receive additional training through seminars and conferences, private studies, internships, etc. Equip them in a way that will benefit the people in their spheres of influence.

2. Maintain a victorious perspective.

Make sure you are prepared to serve and care for people who are struggling with specific problems such as sexual brokenness or addictive behavioral issues. Keep in mind that the groups, teachings and sessions you provide need to be consistent with your philosophy and have a victorious perspective. Remember to think in faith! We are more than overcomers through Him who loved us—that is the simple truth. Because of Jesus, we have authority to release healing. Take steps to recognize and learn the authority you have, so you can do what Jesus did on the earth (see Acts 10:38).

In everything you do, present truth in such a way that those who are hurting can see Jesus and move toward purity and wholeness.

3. Promote your vision for healing regularly.

Preach on the subject of healing on a consistent basis, and encourage people to celebrate those who are taking risks and praying for others. Flood your church with testimonies of healing.

9.5
Healing Ministry Leadership

Focal point: We provide specialized ministry to free people from spiritual bondage.

Steps to building healing ministry leadership:

- Identify
- Recruit (according to destiny)
- Train (on the job with supplementary classroom teaching)
- Deploy (transition them into their new roles with care)
- Support (monitor and nurture)

> *"For I am the Lord who heals you."*
> *— Exodus 15:26*

Every church should have a "hospital" where its members can find healing and restoration. Fill your church with teachings and resources on how to pray for healing, deliverance and comfort, and find people who are actively walking in these things. If possible, try to create income streams for them so they are able to support themselves in this ministry. That is how important it is to have healers readily available to your church body.

As a leader, look at your congregation and see which individuals have a calling for healing. As you preach on the topic, put out the call and see who responds.

- Who in your congregation loves people well?
- Who wants to comfort others?
- Who is known in your church as someone who cares for and nurtures others and brings healing?

The more you can identify these people and begin to pour into them, the more fruitful your ministry will be as a church and the healthier the body will be in general.

For specific steps in how to produce leaders in your church or ministry, please refer to "Raising Up Leaders" in Section 1.5: Apostolic Leadership.

Theme 10
Intergenerational Ministry

We value the partnership of generations for maximum impact.

This theme includes:

- God's heart for intergenerational ministry (Malachi 4:6; 1 Kings 19)
- We help every generation to grow, serve and be served.
- We value all ages for the unique contribution they make.
- We encourage everyone to mentor others and be mentored.
- We connect older and younger leaders to pioneer new ministries together.
- We connect older and younger leaders to minister together.

An Introduction to Intergenerational Ministry

You know how we exhorted, and comforted, and charged every one of you, as a father does his own children, that you would walk worthy of God who calls you into His own kingdom and glory.
— 1 Thessalonians 2:11–12

We live in an individualized society that has embraced this motto: "I can do it by myself." We glorify the self-made man or woman and place a lot of importance on a person's inner strength. But we weren't made to be alone. We weren't made to be people who don't need anyone or anything—we are members of the same body, built to rely on one another. It is time to take a step back and experience biblical, integrous Christianity that sees the Church as God sees it: as a family unit.

At Pastor's Coach, we believe you cannot fully
thrive as a church without intergenerational connection.

As each age group in your church supports, honors, cares for one another and works together in harmony, your church will see Heaven come to earth in a major way.

Intergenerational Ministry and the Culture of Honor

In every church, you will find three age groups:

- Emerging (young) leaders
- Midlevel leaders (people in their 30s and 40s)
- Older leaders

In his first epistle, the apostle John addresses different levels of maturity. He writes to the "children," whose sins are forgiven; to the "young men," who know God's Word and have overcome the wicked one; and finally to the "fathers," who know Him who is from the beginning. Three generations are presented, and each has something incredible to offer the others.

The idea of spiritual generations dovetails with the reality of age. Every church has older and younger saints, spiritual parents and spiritual children. How do you work with all of them? How do you create a sense of synergy between the generations so you can maximize God's purpose?

Your priority is to emphasize a culture of honor.

Sometimes it is unfortunately easy to dishonor those who are older or younger. This almost automatic response can be traced back to the cultural changes of the 1960s, when "generation gap" terminology began to be used. Dishonoring other generations came to be embedded in our society. Many of us have unknowingly perpetuated a legacy of generational brokenness, instead of genuinely appreciating those who belong to a different age group. How do we build churches that foster true honor for each generation?

Remember that every age has something to offer. Look at their unique strengths:

- The older generation gives us strength and wisdom.
- We are carried by the middle generation's power and passion.
- The emerging generation offers innovation and a vital sense of newness.

When we walk in intergenerational partnership, we synthesize wisdom, perseverance and innovation. These elements come together powerfully in new expressions of Kingdom reality that revolutionize the Body of Christ and help us become the Church Jesus wants us to be.

Be sure to communicate to your older believers that they aren't done yet. They make a *huge* difference in your congregation as spiritual grandparents. As a pastor, you have a responsibility to honor the older people in your midst and give them positions of visibility and influence.

Speak with your midlevel and emerging leaders, and establish a mentoring process where there is mutual respect for the generations and appreciation for one another. This allows your church to become a full, thriving expression of Jesus Christ that brings transformation to your region. God calls Himself the God of Abraham, Isaac and Jacob—He is the God of generations.

The Ship Analogy

Intergenerational partnership is similar to a large sailing vessel that has multiple sails and a deep keel. You have a tremendous amount of power to harness the wind…but if you don't have a deep keel, the wind will cause the ship to topple. Unfortunately, a lack of "depth" is why many ministries fail. They have a significant potential for speed, but in many cases, they do not fully possess much-needed elements that usually come with time and experience: wisdom, maturity, discernment, etc. Like the keel of a boat, your older leaders establish a vertical sense of torque. They offer leverage that allows the wind to push hard into the sails without causing the boat to capsize. They have depth, experience and a sense of ballast that give ministries exactly what they're missing.

**Only in intergenerational partnership
can maximum velocity be realized.**

10.1
Vision for Intergenerational Partnership

Focal point: We help every generation to grow, serve and be served.

This focal point includes:

- Intergenerational partnership is God's plan for succession.
- To spread your intergenerational vision, speak about it from the pulpit and model it.
- Create opportunities for younger leaders to be mentored by older leaders in your church.

> *"And he will turn*
> *The hearts of the fathers to the children,*
> *And the hearts of the children to their fathers."*
> *— Malachi 4:6*

As a pastor, you have the main "platform" or voice in your church, which gives you the ability to promote the values you want your church to adopt. This is important to remember as you try to incorporate a vision for intergenerational partnership. What values do you want to instill in your congregation?

Think about your goals concerning intergenerational partnership. What would it look like if the elder body of leaders in your church operated in conjunction with the midlevel and emerging leaders? What would this union produce? It would combine fire, passion and innovation with wisdom, and as it occurred, your church would become a strong community filled with saints of all ages walking together in deep relationship.

To grow that kind of partnership, you need to promote a vision of the different generations walking together in harmony. Scripture is filled with examples of how intergenerational partnership made a huge difference in the overall story of God's purposes in the earth. Give your church pictures of what intergenerational harmony can look like—show them Jesus with the disciples, Moses with Joshua, and Paul with Timothy and Titus.

Intergenerational partnership is God's plan for succession.

It is possible for elder leaders to speak into the lives of emerging leaders in such a way that the emerging leaders can then speak into the next generation. Let's look at one such story found in Scripture.

Elijah and Elisha

In 1 Kings 19, Elijah the prophet was emotionally broken. He had just experienced an incredible victory over the prophets of Baal, but then Queen Jezebel threatened his life and he dropped into a depression.

The Lord spoke to him in a still, small voice: "What are you doing here, Elijah?" Essentially, He was asking, "Why are you depressed?"

The solution God gave Elijah was to mentor the next generation. He told him (this is a paraphrase), "Go find Elisha, put your cloak upon him and raise him up as a prophet in your place." He also told him to raise up Hazael as the next leader in Syria and to anoint a man named Jehu as king over Israel.

Elijah came down off the mountain and found Elisha, who left everything to follow him, and they developed a father-son intergenerational partnership. Elijah did not anoint Hazael himself—Elisha did. Jehu was the next person to be anointed, but Elisha didn't do it…his servant did. Obviously, there is more to the story, but even in this condensed version, we can see how God raises up generations.

As a pastor, you have the power to communicate stories and ideas like these to your people and promote a vision of unity in the generations.

Here are a few ways you can spread intergenerational vision in your church:

1. Speak about it from the pulpit.
2. Model it in the ways you set up your leadership team.

3. Create opportunities for younger leaders to be mentored by older leaders in your church.

As you do these things, the DNA of the Kingdom is passed from generation to generation, and the glory and beauty of Heaven are manifested on earth.

10.2
Culture of Intergenerational Partnership

Focal point: We value all ages for the unique contribution they make.

This focal point includes:

- Your culture is who you are as a church.
- A church becomes steady, strong and unshakeable as wisdom and innovation partner together.
- Know the values and priorities of intergenerational partnership.
- Make intergenerational partnership a daily practice in your church.

> *"But when he was still a great way off, his father saw him and had compassion, and ran and fell on his neck and kissed him."*
> *— Luke 15:20*

One of the keys to a thriving church is making sure members of all ages are valued and that their contribution is respected. As a pastor, you can build a culture that will propel your movement into powerful, amazing synergy.

What do you as a church really care about? What are your values? What drives you? Take a look at your church's values, priorities and practices. Your culture displays who you are. Remember that *culture* is the shared values, priorities and practices, along with the traditions, symbols and expressions, that unite a community. When you know what you care about, you can establish your priorities and be specific about how you spend your time, energy and resources. Out of your priorities, your everyday practices emerge; these are things you do on a daily basis out of habit. Each of these individual "steps" works to establish a *culture of intergenerational partnership* in your church.

If you can build a healthy, strong, cohesive culture at the beginning of the process, you will birth a movement that doesn't necessarily need to be managed.

How to Build a Culture of Healthy Intergenerational Partnership

As you seek to generate a culture of intergenerational partnership, you need to look at the three main components of culture: healthy values, priorities and practices.

1. Values that support intergenerational partnership

What are the values that produce a culture of healthy intergenerational partnership? One is integrity, which allows a church to honor God's purpose for every age level. Another important value is interdependency; a church should value the strength gained through the wisdom of age, as well as the innovation and sense of vitality found in the emerging age group. A church becomes steady, strong and unshakeable as wisdom and innovation partner together.

2. Priorities of intergenerational partnership

How does your church govern its time, energy, money, talents and what you celebrate as a group? How do you allocate your resources? Your answers to these questions reveal your priorities. To make intergenerational partnership a higher priority in your church, talk about it and celebrate it from the pulpit on a regular basis. Bring it to the forefront of people's minds and try to keep it there. Model it yourself, and show your congregation what intergenerational partnership can look like.

3. Make intergenerational partnership a daily practice in your church.

How can you build intergenerational partnership into your church so it becomes a daily practice? One of the main ways you can do this is by making your home and ministry groups inclusive, so they involve different generational levels. Build grandparent leaders into your structures (programs), so they are able to serve and care for the midlevel and younger leaders in a way that produces honor and value for their participation.

Also, it is vital to remind your elder leaders of their importance in the lives of younger leaders. Their lives are not over and their work is not done; they have not lost their value. Scripture holds many *tremendous* examples of elder leaders discipling and mentoring younger ones in a way that produced a culture of true intergenerational partnership. The older generation has strength and wisdom the younger generations desperately need.

We suggest you select a few of your key older leaders and work with them as they spend time with your emerging leaders. For example, those who are grandparents or "empty nesters" could begin to disciple those who still have children in the home.

Remember, culture is the key to leadership. If you can create a strong culture around the values you want your church to embrace, 75 percent of your micro leadership will be done. We encourage you to think strategically and culturally, and create models that show the rest of the congregation how to walk out these principles. In the process, you will be able to revolutionize your congregation and dramatically escalate the Kingdom in your region.

10.3
Lifestyle of Intergenerational Partnership

**Focal point: We encourage everyone to
mentor others and be mentored.**

This focal point includes:

- Make sure your older members do not feel marginalized or irrelevant.
- Give your elder leaders examples of intergenerational partnership.
- Teach your elder leaders how to communicate with younger leaders.
- Practice intergenerational partnership in simple, practical ways.

> *And behold, the Lord stood above it and said: "I am the Lord God of
> Abraham your father and the God of Isaac; the land on which you lie I
> will give to you and your descendants."*
> — Genesis 28:13

Our society constantly communicates, "The older you get, the less relevant you become." It is common for older people to feel more and more marginalized, and we don't want that mindset found anywhere in our churches—the elder community can do some of our best ministry. People over 60 have a *huge* impact on the Body of Christ and the purposes of God for a region.

Let's look at three steps that will help you build a lifestyle of intergenerational partnership in your church:

1. Show your elder leaders what intergenerational partnership looks like and equip them to walk in it.

Make certain the elder members of your congregation know the stories of Moses and Joshua, Paul and Timothy and other leaders in the Bible who made a significant difference in the lives of God's people. Let them know how you, personally, have benefited from mentors.

Give your elder members tools to lead, and raise them up as true mentors. Many of them have professional, ministry and marriage experience that can make a tremendous difference in young leaders' lives. In order for your church to step into the fullness of what God intends, your younger members need the older members, so make sure your elders know they are valued. They have a wealth of information—and much of it wasn't gained through success but failure. As a pastor, value their experience and wisdom and help them feel appreciated.

2. Teach your elder leaders how to communicate.

As you spend time with your elder leaders, speak to them about how to communicate with the younger generation. If older leaders speak insensitively or with a sense of supremacy, they can sabotage the relationships you are hoping they will build. They need to know how to communicate wisdom and experience to the next generation in a way that builds up and strengthens everyone involved.

3. Practice intergenerational partnership.

It may be necessary to bring the older and younger generations together in a room and supervise their interactions. In the partnership you want to initiate, your elder leaders aren't simply disseminating information, but they are also receiving life, vitality and innovation from the emerging generation. As this back-and-forth participation is established as a lifestyle practice, everyone in your church has the means to respect, honor and go to the older generation for wisdom and counsel.

The Best Time of Life

Creating a lifestyle of intergenerational partnership begins as you talk to your older leaders and get them *reactivated*. Ultimately, you want them to initiate relationships through servanthood, love and care that will bring wisdom and depth to your emerging leaders. Help your older leaders reach a place where they are functioning joyfully and with passion.

The grandparent phase is a wonderful season. As you help your older saints understand what spiritual grand-parenting is all about, they will see themselves as an indispensable part of the community. Show your older leaders that the exciting parts of their lives are not over—they are actually in the best time of life right now!

As a pastor, you have the responsibility to create more than a "seniors meeting" in your church. You don't need a seniors meeting—you need a senior army! Build a cohort of senior mentors: a group of passionate leaders who are discussing how they can contribute to the whole body in a way that produces growth and maturity.

10.4
Structures of Intergenerational Partnership

**Focal point: We connect older and younger leaders
to pioneer new ministries together.**

This focal point includes:

- Create hybrid teams.
- Have leaders train up leaders and encourage small groups.
- Make sure you're doing it first; everything you want to bring to your church has to be real inside of you first.

> *And the Lord appeared to him the same night and said, "I am the God of your father Abraham; do not fear, for I am with you. I will bless you and multiply your descendants for My servant Abraham's sake."*
> — *Genesis 26:24*

God is the God of Abraham, Isaac and Jacob—He is the God of generations, and every church needs a plan for helping the generations partner together.

Steps to Building Intergenerational Partnership

1. Create hybrid teams.

Most new ministries will be founded and developed by your younger or midlevel (30s-40s) leaders. To encourage intergenerational partnership, you could make team development part of the standard pioneering process. You could even *require* your pioneers to have an older couple or individual on their teams. That older individual or couple will provide the ballast, strength and depth of wisdom and maturity needed for a new ministry. They may not be the ones in the driver's seat, but they can provide the perspective and overview to help an emerging leader avoid wrong turns. Emerging leaders can be driven by a strong degree of passion or imminent purpose, and the input of a seasoned leader can ward off many mistakes.

At the beginning, intergenerational partnership could be a point of conflict, so it will need to be defined and worked on until it becomes a natural part of your church culture. Make sure harmony exists between younger and older leaders, and work with them to define their unique roles. For instance, in many cases the younger leader is the pioneer and the one making the decisions, yet he needs to be open to the wisdom and counsel of the older leader. Does the older leader understand the kind of counsel and services she can offer? Does she have the power to veto certain decisions made by the younger leader? Make sure everything is clearly defined for your hybrid teams, especially in the beginning.

No matter how much you teach on this topic, nothing can replace your personal coaching as your combined teams pioneer new relationships and blend two age groups in wisdom and harmony.

2. Have leaders train up leaders and encourage small groups.

In every ministry, group or class offered by your church, the leaders should be training up their replacements so the groups can grow and duplicate, and new leaders can be raised up through on-the-job training. If your midlevel and even emerging leaders are training their replacements to honor, respect and learn wisdom from your older leaders, you will have a self-replicating, organic structure that produces strong intergenerational partnership throughout your church body.

Don't neglect the power of small groups as a primary delivery system for every aspect of Christ. Make sure your people are invested in small groups, communicating with each other and processing intergenerational partnership together as a normal part of their Christian life/community experience.

3. Make sure you're doing it first.

If you want your church to be strong in something, you need to be strong in it first. Make intergenerational partnership a priority in your own life. Begin by building it at home and within your staff, and then spread it through your next generation of leaders, so they in turn can promote it with other people in your church.

Make sure your structures are organic and growing from the inside out, so the members of your church can be fully equipped for every good work in Christ. In this way your church will increase and spread to bring transformation to the world around you.

10.5
Intergenerational Leadership

**Focal point: We connect older and younger
leaders to minister together.**

Steps to Building Intergenerational Leadership:

- Identify
- Recruit (according to destiny)
- Train (on the job with supplementary classroom teaching)
- Deploy (transition them into their new roles with care)
- Support (monitor and nurture)

> *And the things that you have heard from me among many witnesses,
> commit these to faithful men who will be able to teach others also.*
> — *2 Timothy 2:2*

How many generations are described in 2 Timothy 2:2? Four, if you count
Paul. Paul was speaking to his son, who would speak to faithful men, who
would teach others also. That is four generations. Paul was essentially saying,
"You've got to guard these things you've seen me do and learned from me.
Pass them on to the next generation—multiply yourself into faithful men,
who will multiply themselves into other people." That is how the Body of
Christ grows. It is the spiritual version of the original commandment given in
Genesis. Do you remember those four amazing statements? *Be fruitful, multiply,
fill the earth, subdue it.* Intergenerational multiplication is God's only plan for
changing the world, and it begins as the different generations choose to
partner together.

Consider these questions:

- How well do you know the older members of your church? What
  could you do to get to know them better?
- How well do you know the younger members of your church? What
  could you do to get to know them better?

- How could you train the different generations to work together and rely on one another? What sort of events could you plan? What structures could you build?

We live in a world that separates the generations, so we have to swim against the tide to bring generational unity. Make certain members of all ages feel valued and that their contribution is respected. When your leaders are raising up their trainees to respect and rely on the wisdom of other generations, you will be replicating intergenerational ministry in a healthy way.

For specific steps in how to produce leaders in your church or ministry, please refer to "Raising Up Leaders" in Section 1.5: Apostolic Leadership.

For More Information

Thank you for joining us! If you have questions about any of the points included in this book, or if you would like more information about building your church, developing leaders and small groups, creating culture, launching new churches and ministries, etc., visit our website at www.PastorsCoach.com and sign up for one of our subscription packages.

Pastor's Coach offers a variety of resources for pastors and ministry leaders, and we are constantly adding more material and helpful products to our online library. We specialize in personal coaching both for individual pastors and leader; and leadership teams; contact us at info@pastorscoach.com to inquire about coaching.

To receive a free email newsletter delivering tips, teachings and updates about Pastor's Coach and our products, register directly at www.PastorsCoach.com.

In whatever way Pastor's Coach can support you in the future, please let us know. May the Lord bless you and keep you as you travel the exciting road ahead!

Other Books by Michael Brodeur Include:

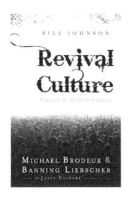

Revival Culture: Prepare for the Next Great Awakening
Featuring Banning Liebscher and Bill Johnson (Baker Publishing Group, Chosen Books)

Destiny Finder A Practical Approach to Unlocking Your Destiny
Forward by Banning Liebscher (Quintessant Media)

Visit us at:

www.pastorscoach.com and www.destinyfinder.com.

27477352R00108

Made in the USA
Columbia, SC
30 September 2018